Journeys Through Time

Journeys Through Time

Uncovering my past lives

Jenny Cockell

PIATKUS

PIATKUS

First published in Great Britain in 2008 by Piatkus Books

A CIP catalogue record for this book
is available from the British Library

ISBN 978-0-7499-0969-7

Typeset in Bembo by Phoenix Photosetting, Chatham, Kent
www.phoenixphotosetting.co.uk
Printed and bound in Great Britain by
MPG Books, Bodmin, Cornwall

Papers used by Piatkus Books are natural, renewable and recyclable
products made from wood grown in sustainable forests and certified
in accordance with the rules of the Forest Stewardship Council

Mixed Sources
Product group from well-managed
forests and other controlled sources
www.fsc.org Cert no. SGS-COC-004081
© 1996 Forest Stewardship Council
FSC

Piatkus Books
An imprint of
Little, Brown Book Group
100 Victoria Embankment
London EC4Y 0DY

An Hachette Livre UK Company
www.hachettelivre.co.uk

www.piatkus.co.uk

Contents

Acknowledgements

I would like to thank the many people without whose extensive help and enthusiasm this journey would not have been possible, in particular Hisayo Funakoshi, Jim Alexander and Brian Thomas. I also want to thank all those people in both Ireland and Japan who generously gave up their time to provide information and answer my questions, with especial gratitude to the descendants of Samurai Hanafusa. Finally, a warm thank you to my husband Steve, who has put up with many years of my involvement with past lives with good humour and endless support.

Dedicated to the memory of Sonny Sutton, 1919–2002

Introduction

Since my earliest childhood, I have had memories of my past lives – not just one or two, but many. Some of these have so haunted me that I have been driven to delve deeper into my memories and search for the truth of their origins. This book tells the story of my search.

When I first embarked on this research, I was hesitant to discuss it openly. Belief in reincarnation used to be considered an oddity, confined to Eastern religions but not to be taken seriously in the West. Nowadays, however, although it is still a difficult idea for many Westerners to accept, attitudes towards reincarnation are becoming more open and many people are reconsidering their ideas about death and the continuity of life. Popular television programmes have helped to spread the concept, and there is a growing body of serious research that suggests that reincarnation is a reality that can in some cases be proved. Not only do numbers of people remember their past lives, but on occasion their memories have been backed up by external evidence. The laws of nature tend to be consistent. Therefore, if there is sufficient evidence that some people remember past lives, it would be reasonable to believe that everyone has lived before.

There are two main ways of demonstrating the reality of reincarnation. One is when evidence can be found to support the accounts of people who have described past lives under hypnosis. The most convincing demonstration, however, is the increasing number of children who talk spontaneously about past-life memories from an early age, and are able to give specific details of those lives that can be checked out.

There are numerous documented cases of children whose descriptions of previous lives have been verified; a number of these children – many of them in India – have been able to contact and recognise their former families. Most of the work of research and documentation has been undertaken since 1960 by the late Professor Ian Stevenson of the University of Virginia, and in India since 1979 by Dr Satwant Pasricha, author of *Claims of Reincarnation* (1990). By the time of his death in 2007, Dr Stevenson had more than three thousand cases on his files.

In *The Children That Time Forgot* (1983), an Englishwoman, Mary Harrison, describes how she placed an advertisement in a women's magazine asking for mothers to contact her if they had had any odd experiences with young children. Expecting to collect light-hearted anecdotes, she received hundreds of letters about children reporting details of previous lives. The most common phrase they used was 'when I was here before'. The stories they told were consistent in their detail and unchanged with each retelling, despite the youth of the children concerned.

Although a detailed past-life memory is still not very common, most children have fragments of memory from their previous lives. The brainwaves of children under six are slightly different from those of older children and adults, and similar to those achieved through meditation. This may be why the recall is easier at that age, and also why small children are more likely to see spirits, often explained away as 'imaginary friends'. But, whether the recall is vague or quite detailed, these memories almost universally fade as the child grows up, and by the age of seven are usually completely forgotten. I believe that this is how things are meant to be. We are not meant to remember our previous lives, but to live the current life to the full.

But this is not the case for everyone. A small but significant number of people never quite forget their past lives. I am one of these people. One reason children remember past lives has been brought to light in Dr Satwant Pasricha's work: these memories are particularly likely to be recalled when the previous life ended early and suddenly, leaving behind unfinished business. In my own case, that is part of the answer: the two lives that have affected me most deeply both ended early, leaving me with a sense of guilt that I brought with me into this life. But it is not the whole answer. I was also a quiet, introspective child, coping with a difficult home life, and apparently I did not entirely relinquish the meditative state of mind when I grew beyond six years old.

My past-life memories are, on the whole, exactly the same in nature as any other memory. Though I recalled some particular events in dreams, this was not the case for most of my past-life knowledge. In the early days of my research I did find it easier to explain the memories in terms of dreams. Some people found this more acceptable and less disturbing than the truth, which is that on a day-to-day basis I had memories stretching back over many lives and thousands of years.

Although I could remember snatches of a number of lifetimes, there were four memories that predominated. One was very recent: my life as Mary Sutton, a young Irishwoman who died in childbirth in her thirties, which haunted me for many years. Next in importance was the life that I always knew was immediately prior to Mary's, as a young girl in nineteenth-century Japan. Then there was a rather lonely life as Anna, a servant in eighteenth-century France. The last life that was important to me took place very long ago, as a young man in Neolithic times; this was a truly happy memory.

The most overwhelming of these was the life that ended twenty-one years before my birth: the life of Mary Sutton, who died in the 1930s shortly after giving birth to her eighth child. My long search for the children Mary left behind culminated in my finding her family, and is described in the first part of this book, based on my book *Yesterday's Children* (Piatkus Books, 1993). At the time, seeking the identity of the person I had been in a previous life seemed a very strange task, yet, despite being beset by self-doubt, deep down I knew that the memories and emotions relating to that time were real.

The enthusiasm that greeted *Yesterday's Children* took me aback, but justified all my hard work. Although my quest to find my past life was private and personal, my story resonated with many readers, who perhaps had had similar experiences that they found hard to talk about, and were reassured that they were not alone. For me, the cathartic effect of tracing my past-life family was like emerging into the light after years of walking in the shadows. It encouraged me to continue writing about my other experiences.

As well as my memories of the past, I had always had other psychic experiences – strong instances of telepathy, for example, and glimpses of the future, many of which came about. These sporadic visions made a sudden leap while I was still trying to trace Mary's children, when I found myself having a totally clear sense of myself as a child in the next century. I knew that the future could not be ignored, that I had to look further into this extraordinary experience. In my explorations of the future, although they are hard to explain and verify, I found enough consistent features to be able to take an overall view from the available fragments. This view I was able to share in my second book, *Past Lives, Future Lives* (Piatkus Books, 1996), which I have also drawn from here.

In my teens I had a powerful premonition that there would be two important phases in my life; these would include troubles and difficulties, but would ultimately bring me greater peace of mind. The first phase coincided with my search for Mary Sutton's family. The second, lasting between my forty-ninth and fifty-fourth years, has only recently ended. In 2002 I began the hard task of researching the life before Mary's, a very different life as a young Japanese girl living and dying in the late nineteenth century. This story is told for the first time here.

I do not revel in public exposure, but at the same time I feel strongly that I can contribute to normalising the concept of reincarnation by sharing an accurate record of my own story. As a child I was shocked to discover that people saw reincarnation as simply a belief. For me it was the only explanation for my personal memories of past lives. However, the attitude of other people made me realise the necessity of tolerance towards different viewpoints.

It is not my object to change anyone's beliefs. But I hope that, by demonstrating that my own memories are real, I can give reassurance to those of you who are perhaps troubled or confused by memories of past lives. If you doubt yourself, or have met with scepticism, I hope that this book will give you the confidence to trust in your own experience. You may also wish to explore your memories further; whether or not you take this course, I have found that, ultimately, we need to accept the past, learn from it what we need to, and move on to live life now to the full.

When answering people's questions, I have always tried to present as clear and truthful a picture as possible; for me, information based on experience is worth a thousand theories. It is my personal story that I offer you. If there are any conclusions to be drawn from my experiences, the most important are that we are eternal, spiritual beings, for whom life is continuous, and that, at soul level, we are all connected parts of a greater whole.

CHAPTER 1

A Haunted Childhood

I grew up haunted by memories of the past and by the guilt and confusion that some of them carried with them. Some of these memories came to me in dreams, but most came in the same way as anyone remembers a past event, and I took them for granted – troubling though some of them were. I also had glimpses of the future, and could sense the feelings of others through telepathy. Until I was four I had no idea that these were not ordinary experiences.

My background was ordinary enough. I was born in Barnet, Hertfordshire, in 1953; a year later my family moved to a new housing area on the edge of St Albans. My father was a rising electronics engineer, my mother a housewife. It was not a happy household: my father's dark moods and anger affected us all. I had two brothers, Michael, who was a year older than I was, and Alan who was four years younger. We enjoyed a semi-rural setting, as the estate nestled against open countryside and woodland, where I loved to walk. I also enjoyed watching the last steam trains from my window and their distant carriage lights outlining the dark horizon on winter nights. My pleasure in both the countryside and the trains was coloured by their echoes of earlier existences.

I knew that I had lived in the countryside in several past lives and that my love of trains was linked to a memory of Ireland.

Somehow I have always felt certain of the period covered by my previous lives; in Mary Sutton's case I knew that her life spanned a period roughly from 1898 to the 1930s, so that she would have died quite young. I also knew that she had lived and died in Ireland. My childhood dreams were swamped by memories of Mary's death. I remembered being in a large room with white walls; a tall, multi-paned window almost opposite me let in a great deal of light. I knew that I had been ill for a while, possibly weeks, but by now the physical pain had become remote. I had difficulty breathing, though: each breath was an effort, which in itself induced panic. There was also a fever, which brought with it a distortion of thought and my perception of time. The only certainty was that I was alone and near death in a place that was not home.

All this, however, was unimportant beside my fear for the children I was leaving behind. I wanted to fight death, to avoid that final separation – but death came, inevitably and repeatedly, in my dreams, and I would wake in tears. It was too soon to go, much too soon to leave the children. And somehow I felt it was my fault. I knew I had escaped from a bad situation, through no fault of my own, but I had left the children behind and my sense of guilt was powerful. I was filled with a confusion of emotions that would have been difficult for an adult to cope with. But I kept my tears to myself; a rather withdrawn child, I felt that the grief was too private to speak of, even to my mother.

Happier memories of Mary's life often came to me during

the day. The strongest concerned the children. I could remember an older son who was perhaps thirteen and getting quite tall. He was a little soldier, confident, very open and straightforward, a good judge of situations and not afraid of being gentle. The oldest girl had long hair and a thick fringe; quiet at times, she was patient, willing and helpful – I remembered her going to fetch water from a pump or a spring – and she was clever, doing well at school. I felt particularly guilty about her, since she would have to look after the others after my death, which would mean giving up her school work.

Then there were at least two more boys. The elder was energetic with a relentless sense of humour, while his slightly younger brother was quieter, perhaps a little secretive. A younger girl, who I felt was no more than five, was very pretty and feminine, with blonde hair and blue eyes. And there was a very small boy who would run his hand absent-mindedly along the hem of his jacket, fidgeting with his clothes; he was very quiet, something of a loner. I felt he was a child one could not help but like, but who was uneasy with too much show of affection – I remembered wanting to hug him, but knowing that would make him feel smothered.

I felt that there was one younger child, and that there were seven or eight in all, though I was not certain about the details. But I must have remembered the blonde child in particular, for my favourite childhood doll had slightly curly blonde hair. It had an ingenious mechanism that enabled the eyes to change colour, but I always kept them at blue. This doll remains in my possession, dressed in baby clothes, to this day.

There was a sense of guilt, too, about my life in Japan.

Like Mary's life, this came to me in glimpses, less often than Mary's, and it took me a while to build up a final picture. It seemed to have been a pleasant life, in a well-to-do family. We lived in a house with a veranda, overlooking the sea. I knew that I had died by drowning at the age of seventeen. I had fallen off a ferry on the way to marry the man my father had chosen for me and I felt some responsibility about this. I was brought up with the traditional Japanese woman's sense of duty, and by my death I had let my father down, had failed in my duty to him, especially as I sensed there may have been something intentional about the manner of my death. There was sadness, too: I loved my home and did not want to leave it for marriage to a stranger. I wanted to be able to stand on the veranda once more looking out, preferably on a wet and stormy day when the wind blew and sea churned and I could feel full of life.

My past-life memories had an influence on my behaviour and activities. For example, when my older brother wanted me to play soldiers with him I would agree to join in only if he would let me be either Irish or Japanese. If I was being Japanese I felt I should be strong, loyal and reserved, which was how I remembered my father in that life. I would use a stick as a sword, rather than a gun. When my brother told me to hide and try to ambush him, I would refuse; I didn't think my Japanese father was likely to hide – it seemed cowardly – and I refused to use a toy gun. In the end my brother would lose patience with me and play with my younger brother instead.

In fact, I wasn't especially keen on childhood games. What I really enjoyed was cleaning and tidying. My toys were kept neatly in boxes, which I labelled as soon as I could write, and my clothes were always carefully folded and stacked. This was partly so that I would be ready to move out when my parents decided to separate – which I knew would happen at some point – but I also took pleasure in the act of cleaning itself. I liked sweeping the wooden floor of our garden shed with a broom, just as Mary would sweep her hard stone floor. This was not a game – I would do the job thoroughly, even when I was quite young. The activities of tidying and sweeping also resonated with my life in Japan, when I loved doing the chores in my ocean-side home, using a flat hand brush made of reeds attached in a fan shape.

I would get angry at my thick, bushy hair, which did not behave as it had in any past life I could remember, and I did not like it cut short. In Japan it had been sleek and long, and I thought that, if I grew it, it would become the right sort of hair, but my mother would not let me. Mary's hair was also long, and seemed slightly wavy. I was at least school age before I realised that the hair I had was mine for this life, and wasn't going to change!

★　★　★

Of the senses, one of the greatest aids to past-life memory is that of smell. This is likely to be because the area in the brain where smell is interpreted is next door to the area for memory, and there are a number of connections that go directly from one centre to the other without going through any conscious control. So strong is the connection that I am sure that many people would find it a useful trigger to past-life memory. If a particular smell kindles odd or unexpected feelings, it is worth making a note of and exploring those feelings.

All four of my strongest past-life memories were linked to the smell of the sea. Mary Sutton lived a few hundred yards from an estuary mouth; Anna, the French servant, lived mostly in a port town, and the pre-Celtic life took place within walking distance of the coast. Often in the evening I would gaze out of my bedroom window for hours at the countryside beyond the rooftops. In stormy weather, when water ran down the road outside in torrents, I would imagine I was looking out at the wild sea from the veranda of my Japanese home.

All through my childhood I would try hard to see views like those I had seen before, and, partly for that reason, I especially liked trips to the seaside. Yet, although I enjoyed paddling, I was very nervous about learning to swim; I was terrified of getting out of my depth or getting my face wet. Water reminded me of my drowning; if my face went under I would panic and imagine I could see frightened faces above, trying to reach for me as I spiralled downward.

I did learn to swim eventually, but only because when I was ten my father dug a small swimming pool in the garden for us to play in, so that he didn't have to take us on holiday. I could go in at five or six on a summer morning, when I could be alone in the icy water with no other children to splash me. The water was very shallow, and the pool was small, so I learned to swim without getting my face wet or getting out of my depth. But I never completely got over my fear, and hated having my head completely covered by water, which gave my mother quite a problem when she had to wash my hair.

Some of my difficulties arose from a combination of my many memories. For example, I never felt comfortable in any of my clothes. I had never worn short skirts in any previous life, and they always felt wrong. However, I loved the freedom of wearing trousers. It reminded me of the oldest of my memories, of being a Neolithic hunter on his first lone hunt, which was a rite of passage for accession to manhood. The memories from that life had a sense of freedom and adventure that I was happy to allow to spill over into the present. I would dress in scruffy, boyish attire and tramp through woodland, taking the spirit of my life as a hunter with me. I would reach the old pond on the other side and hunt for wildlife in its muddy banks, happy if I found only a few insects or a frog.

The joy of that Neolithic memory remained a part of my present personality from childhood on. Whenever I needed courage and energy, I could draw on that life for physical challenges; I would always equate energetic enthusiasm with the sense of inner calm and freedom I experienced then, thousands of years ago.

I had no cause to doubt that my memories were real and I assumed that everyone had similar experiences. The first time I had any idea that my view of reality was different from other people's was when I started going to Sunday school with my older brother. I was nearly four, not yet at day school, and had as yet no real understanding of life outside my home. It felt strange sitting on the floor at the front of a crowd of children in the old Scout hut, a musty-smelling building that lacked proper heating. Here I daydreamed, taking in my surroundings rather than listening to what was going on.

I did prick up my ears one day, however, when someone began talking to us about death and what happened afterwards. Miss Barrand, the district nurse who ran the Sunday school, had introduced a solidly built man in a suit who was talking about heaven. I was very concerned that he made no mention of past lives. Assuming that such memories were common, I had already begun to wonder why nobody ever mentioned them. I couldn't understand how this man could talk about subjects like death and heaven without including other lives, past or future.

Afterwards, I sat on the tall stool in the kitchen, talking with my mother. She asked me if I had enjoyed it: I had — there was a comforting feeling about the singing and the earnest discussion. But I told her I couldn't understand why they never mentioned past lives. Although at the time my mother didn't believe in life after death, she showed no surprise or disbelief; she responded carefully, explaining that reincarnation was a belief, not an accepted fact. She always respected my individuality, and her considerate attitude was a great support to me during the rest of my childhood. Nevertheless, this revelation was a shock to me, causing me to worry and constantly question myself. Adults generally knew more than children, and I didn't want to be wrong. Soon afterwards I found out that other people, particularly other children, were disbelieving or at least puzzled when I talked about past lives.

It was some years later, when I was about eight, that I discovered that I was different in other ways. Most people, it seemed, did not dream about events before they happened, as I did. Again, I thought premonition was normal, and I had no doubts about it because very often my premonitions were confirmed within a few weeks. From that point on I decided that adults were not always right, and I would not allow other people's views to create doubts in my mind about things I knew to be real. Nonetheless, I learned to be careful about whom I talked to of these experiences, and to keep some things to myself. I would discuss 'unusual' things only with my mother, whom I could trust. As a result I became rather introverted.

When I was nine, as well as going to Sunday school I began to attend Bible-study classes with my older brother and a friend. I soon became disenchanted with the conventional religious ideas we were taught. I had very clear ideas of my own and felt unable to compromise. Later, I looked into other religions and was delighted when the school curriculum was altered to include comparative religion. But, although I found more in Eastern beliefs to match my views, I still found all religious teaching constricting. I could not see God as a separate, overseeing entity. My idea of 'God' was – and still is – more like an energy that includes all living things and of which we are all a part.

Although I was quiet, I made friends fairly easily at school, but was never one of the gang and tended to spend much time alone. However, until I was seven, the people I regarded as my closest friends were quite different. Many children have imaginary friends; but my 'imaginary friends' were totally real to me, although no one else could see them. They looked quite solid and talked with me; I knew they were people who had actually lived, though I never thought of them as ghosts. When I wanted them to be with me, I was able to go into an altered state of consciousness, a kind of trance, and they would appear.

They were friends, and I felt they had been friends in past lives. One was a young man, perhaps in his early twenties, wearing army uniform from the Second World War. His constant talking and joking could at times be irritating, and I preferred to talk with his companion, an older, quieter man, with a deep, soft voice and a lot of patience. We regularly held long conversations, communicating mentally, and although I don't remember our talks in detail they were very comforting and important. Best of all, they listened to me. We spoke of feelings and matters of a more spiritual nature; the older man would advise me on how to be true to myself, and not let others try to change the person inside.

I was very upset when one day my friends told me they would not be able to return. We were in the playground at primary school, and were all three sitting on a wall surrounding a small planted patch of ground. When I asked them why, they said something about its being time to move on and for me to grow up some more, which I didn't really understand. The teacher blew the whistle, and they were still there as I looked back while we filed into the classroom. That was my last sight of them, sitting on the wall, waving and smiling.

I missed them deeply. It was the first time I had experienced any sort of loss or grief in my present life, and I tried to call them back a few times without success. After that I did begin to grow up a bit; I spent less time in a state of trance and concentrated more on the world that everybody could see.

Even as a small child I would spend some time each day in a withdrawn, meditative state. This was more than childish daydreaming: it was my gateway to a spiritual and psychic awareness that I continued to think of as perfectly normal. It also became my escape mechanism from stress at home, which was not a happy place. There an impossible tension between my parents, and life was often darkened by my father's moods.

My father was a fit, imposing giant of a man. He was very quiet most of the time, though when he felt communicative he had a knack of explaining complex ideas in a few succinct words. Sometimes he would be troubled and moody for long spells, and his anger could be terrifying. My brothers, my mother and I learned to cope by avoidance, and my later childhood years, particularly between eight and thirteen, have been partially suppressed. I do remember my older brother Michael receiving a number of severe beatings, as did my younger brother Alan on occasion.

Perhaps the atmosphere at home caused me to immerse myself in my memories of Mary, though it is impossible to know which was the greater: the fear within family life, or the torment of the dream and dying over and over again, knowing that I was deserting the children. I once tried to change the ending of the dream, as one might an ordinary nightmare, but I knew I could not change something that was already history. I woke that night in floods of tears, and an even greater awareness of the reality of that dream.

I was a child with the feelings of both a child and an adult, and this made enormous demands on my emotions. Rendered even more vulnerable by the aggression at home, I would dream even in the classroom. When Michael started school his teacher was worried because he was so far ahead of the rest of his class, and in common with several of our relatives he was found to have a genius-level IQ. My teachers, by contrast, were concerned because I appeared to be slow or lazy. No one seemed to consider changing those labels to read 'highly stressed' or to investigate what was going on. I was easily upset; I feared punishment if I made a mistake and was terrified if the teachers shouted at anyone.

When I was eight a routine IQ test showed that I was actually much brighter than my school work had led everyone to believe. I was moved into a top group, but was so afraid of getting things wrong that I would compulsively check my answers again and again, which of course slowed me down. It is only quite recently that I discovered that I have a form of dyslexia, which cannot have helped.

I sometimes wonder how many people forget their past lives. If I had not repeatedly looked at my memories and kept them clear, might they all have faded, leaving behind only the feelings of guilt? Or was my daydreaming as much to do with the need to remember as with the avoidance of my present life? Perhaps the two were interrelated. Perhaps, too, my constant focus on thoughts of the past helped to preserve them. I felt I had to hold onto my memories of Mary in the secret hope that one day I might be able to resolve my torment about the children.

Throughout my childhood I would escape into my recollections of Mary's children and our home in Ireland. I had vivid memories of our cottage and of walking along the lane next to it. The cottage was small, built of buff-coloured stone. Above the solid wooden door, the roof – which was possibly slate – sagged noticeably and the few small windows did not let in much light. There were no stairs, so I assumed it was single-storey, and although there were very few rooms I remember one or two small attached outbuildings.

The kitchen, running the depth of the cottage from front to back, was very cramped and dark. Mary spent much of her time here cooking, which seemed to involve a lot of boiling on something completely unfamiliar to me as a child – a kitchen range of a type I did not see until adulthood. She also regularly made round flat loaves, mixing flour with her hands. I would echo this in childhood play, mixing grass seeds with water.

Mary's cottage marked the beginning of a small hamlet of perhaps ten to twelve homes, mainly strung along the same side of the lane – most of the other side consisted of boggy meadows unsuitable for building on. To the rear, beyond a small vegetable patch, was woodland. I loved the rural environment and that love spilled over from one life to the next; my childhood was filled with woodland walks. I often sought out free and wild places.

The nearby village I remembered in detail. We always went there on foot; as Mary, I remember walking with the children to church, and alone when going shopping. I felt there were shops on a north-to-south road in the middle of the village, where there was also a small church. From this road it was possible to see a large pair of wooden gates on the opposite side of the main road and to the right of the junction; these had some significance. The railway station was set back from the main road, which ran along the top of the village in an arc. Mary had some interest in steam trains – I didn't know why – and I often dreamed about them, but couldn't remember travelling on them. I knew that the village lay north of a major city that was probably too far to walk to.

I always felt that Mary was Catholic. Although there were occasional trips to the city without the children, and others in the opposite direction, the main outings were to church. At least I presumed they were to church, because the whole family were present and dressed in Sunday best.

(When I myself was young I used to dress up on Sundays. When asked why, I would simply say, 'Because it's Sunday.' This made perfect sense to me, even though my family were not churchgoers.) Some other adults came too, including a female friend who seemed to be close. She used to stand and talk as Mary worked in the kitchen – she talked a lot! At some point in time the name of Molly, or something similar, became attached to the memory of this friend.

It took me years to realise that Mary's husband was present on these outings to church. He seemed to be a taciturn man, seldom around, although there were flashes of a younger and happier person, who was very important to Mary. But my memories of him were unclear, shifting from one vague picture to another, almost as though I was trying to block them out.

At lot of the remembering came in isolated fragments and sometimes I would have difficulty making sense of them. Other parts were complete and very detailed. It was something like a jigsaw, with certain pieces faded and others mislaid, but enough of them present and clear enough to give a fair overall whole. Memories of the children predominated, as did the cottage and its setting; other places and people were less precise. There was a smallish black dog, for instance, which must have belonged to the children, since I don't remember walking it. There were farm animals near the cottage, and I seemed to remember an animal that was trapped.

Among other, smaller, fragmented memories that were hard to place in time was one of myself as Mary, standing on a small wooden jetty at dusk, waiting for a boat to come – though whom I was waiting for I could never remember. I wore a dark shawl, which failed to keep out the cold wind.

There were also thoughts about Mary's father and two older brothers, who seemed to have gone away. Her relationship with her father was warm. A gentle, humorous man, he dressed untidily in old clothes, and I felt that some of his work involved looking after the fields. My memory of and feelings about Mary's mother were vaguer and less powerful. The older brother was gentle, with a deep soft voice. The younger had a wiry build and endless energy; he was always joking and smiling. It was not until my late teens that I connected them with my two childhood friends; their characters were very similar.

Perhaps not surprisingly, I still find it hard to see Mary herself, but I feel her personality and remember her clothes. She had a preference for blouses with sleeves gathered into a band just below the elbow – I still find myself rolling up my shirt sleeves, or actually sewing up the wrist bands of blouses – and I recall a long, dark, woollen skirt. When I was a child, my skirts always felt too short for comfort, and the fabric was too light.

There were worries, too. There never seemed to be enough money to buy much food, and although vegetables may have been grown in the patch next to the cottage, I felt that either the vegetables or the patch in some sense did not belong to us. I also associated shopping with market stalls down one side of a cobbled street that ended with a postbox on the corner. Behind the stalls were shops, much too expensive to buy goods from. The market stalls sold a variety of goods, including vegetables, fresh fish and sometimes meat. Some sold clothing, which may have been second-hand, and there were one or two selling household items. The whole scene was busy, and the point of being there was to find

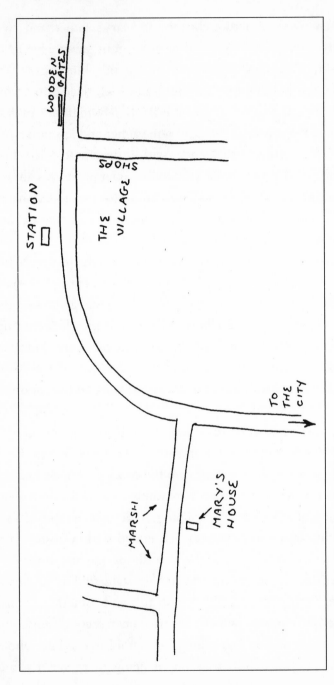

Map of Mary's village, first drawn in childhood

bargains. I don't remember actually buying very much. What was confusing, though, was that this market did not seem to be in the village, however hard I tried to place it there.

I was fairly good at drawing, and would repeatedly draw rough maps of Mary's village, marking the shops, the main roads, the station and her home. I started making these maps around the age of eight or nine while at junior school, pretty much as soon as I could understand what maps were about. Sometimes, other remembered landmarks would appear, but my maps were remarkably consistent over the years.

One day, I decided that, if I could look at a map of Ireland, I would know where Mary's village was located, and would be able to match it with my own maps. The only map I could find was in my school atlas, with the whole of Ireland on just one page, so it was unlikely that I would be able to find a match. I decided to try anyway. I sat with the atlas page in front of me, then shut my eyes for a few moments to let memory take over. I tried this several times, and each time I was drawn back to the same spot. Mary, I felt sure, must have seen maps, or I would not have been able to draw my own. The place I was being drawn to was called Malahide, and it was just north of Dublin. I drew these maps out of the need to know where I had lived, as I was certain that one day I would go back there – although at the time I had no idea how.

CHAPTER 2
Growing Up

At home, things did not improve. Despite our careful behaviour, my brothers and I were constantly attracting our father's wrath. We would be lined up after any minor misdemeanour and questioned in turn, though we were usually too terrified to speak. My father would then decide who was guilty, and beat the selected culprit. One of the worst times was when I ate five marshmallows from an open packet and my father decided that Michael was responsible. I felt terribly guilty about the beating that should have come to me. I tried to apologise to Michael as he lay writhing on his bed in tears; we had been very close until then, but this event strained our relationship severely for a long time to come.

Some people could sense my fear and recognised me as a potential victim, and I became a target for bullying at school, but by the age of ten I was learning how to fight back. At home I was helpless, but I was not going to let anyone outside frighten me. I also tried to protect my brothers. I took part in a series of mock fights with boys from among my friends, one of them culminating in a bleeding nose for my opponent. As a result, I gained a reputation for toughness, and my presence alone was enough to protect my brothers.

My school work improved as I began to be more awake to the present, and I gained a place at grammar school. But I did not begin to achieve anything like my full potential until I was thirteen, when my parents finally separated. Until then I was still dreaming, sometimes about the past – almost always about Mary and Ireland – sometimes about the future. I had always known that my parents would separate, and had packed and repacked my belongings for departure many times, so when it happened I was not surprised. But, although it was a huge relief, by the time my mother, brothers and I moved out, I had fallen into a pattern of regular deep depressions. There would be months on end when I found it hard to concentrate, alternating with bouts of almost obsessive enthusiasm, usually for a creative or artistic project.

We left with virtually nothing and had to stay for a while with family friends. Despite this, my school work continued to improve and I began to find it easier to be sociable. For a year or so there was little time to spend alone thinking, and Mary took a back seat in my mind. Then my mother was given two rooms in a large house with a job as housekeeper which she somehow combined with full-time adult education. By the time I was fifteen, she had managed to raise a private mortgage on a large, decrepit old house. We acquired a lodger and at last embarked on a life that felt worth living. The house was always full of people, and it was a happy time.

Although I was unhappy and isolated at secondary school, I began to develop a full social life outside. I joined youth groups and a folk-dance group; I enjoyed anything to do with the countryside and exercise, from charity walks to canoeing and camping trips.

Now that I was more settled, I was able once again to think about Mary and the children, and found that somehow my desperation had changed to optimism. This was the 1960s, when people were becoming more open-minded, and I found it easier to talk openly about psychic matters, and about Mary. I needed to externalise and face some of my suppressed emotions – though just how much emotion had been suppressed I did not yet realise. I was able to confide my fears about the children, and the positive reactions of my friends gave me confidence. I began to see my tentative thoughts of proving my memories of Mary to be true as a quest to be fulfilled.

With limited money and no car, I knew this quest would have to wait. I also knew that I needed first to understand myself and my feelings. For I would still drift off into my private trance world, and was still subject to the dark depression that would grip me with no apparent cause. (Later this was diagnosed as a metabolic problem that I may have inherited from my father.)

My mother, meanwhile, progressed through teacher training into teaching, and eventually postgraduate training. While teaching, she made a friend whose husband was a member of the St Albans Morris Dancers. For the first time I was exposed to music that I really enjoyed, and listening to traditional Irish music felt like coming home. When I first heard the sound of an unaccompanied Gaelic voice, a door seemed to open into a different, older world, which held a strange sense of mystery and beauty. I was sure that Mary had enjoyed music like this.

At one point I borrowed a flute from one of the Morris musicians; in a week I had learned to play a couple of tunes on it. Then I cut some bamboo to make a six-holed flute of my own. I had no idea at the time that what I had made was very similar to a traditional Japanese flute.

At sixteen I escaped from school and went to study for A-levels at a college of further education; here I spent two very happy years and found it easier to make friends. I even found myself getting on better with my father; on Sundays he used to play at a jazz club, where I was able to talk with him. I had already learned after we left home that he was actually gay. At this time, homosexuality was still illegal and discovery could have cost him his job. This explained his dark moods and unhappy marriage, and I was able to feel some compassion for his problems, and the beginnings of forgiveness. Talking with him at the jazz club, I gradually began to understand his own bleak childhood and the inner pain that gave rise to his anger. There, too, I met his partner Roland, and realised that my father was happy. I had never seen him happy before.

I was beginning to open up all round, and my interest in various psychic phenomena began to grow. Not only did memories of my past lives recur regularly, but so did glimpses of the future. Many of my shorter-term premonitions turned out to be accurate, and I began taking notice of my visions of the more distant future.

One of these really worried me. It took the form of an extremely complex and disturbing dream in which I saw myself in my mid-thirties going through some kind of crisis – of what kind was not clear. During one scene I could see my worried expression as I arrived somewhere in an estate car accompanied by two fair-haired children. I also knew that once this crisis was over something would happen to change my life, after which I would have no more major worries. It was many years before I was to understand what this dream was about.

I experienced an increase in a number of minor phenomena, often in the form of telepathy, particularly with family members. Most instances of telepathy occurred spontaneously, but in my mid-teens I began to experiment more deliberately by sending thought messages. Once, delayed on a journey home, I sent the thought, 'I'm all right, Mum, but I'll be a bit late.' When I got back, my mother said, 'I knew you were all right – you told me.' I tried sending mental instructions to animals, and I found that a dog will respond and do as you ask, whereas a cat will understand and embark on the activity – and then refuse to go on.

It seems that animals can also communicate with us, if we are receptive. My favourite pet was a grass snake, given to me by a friend when I was sixteen. It had been very nervous of people and known to bite, but gradually we built up a trusting relationship and it never bit anyone again. One Saturday morning I had a premonition that I didn't at first associate with my pet. I was wide awake and the vision was very vivid. I saw a friend of my mother's and her children, and I felt as if I myself were dead and under water. Strangely, this feeling was not frightening but totally calm and loving. It was puzzling, because I was sure I wasn't about to die.

That afternoon my mother's friend called unexpectedly and I introduced her children to the snake. When I returned it to its tank it slid lifelessly into the shallow water trough, and I realised that it had died quietly in my hands. I believe that the snake had known it was going to die, and wanted me to understand that this was nothing to be sad about. The loss of my pet was tempered by the tremendously uplifting experience we had shared in my vision, and I had no need to mourn.

After that I would sometimes know when people were going to die. There seemed to be no pattern to these knowings, and they didn't occur with everyone, but if I foresaw a death it always happened. I never told anyone about these premonitions.

When I was sixteen I had a major experience that has had a long-lasting influence on my beliefs and philosophy. One very still and mild evening in the late summer of 1969 I was walking home from a friend's house. As I passed the remains of the defensive ditch built outside St Albans in Roman times, there was little traffic along the road. A light breeze rustled in the many trees overhanging the pavement. My brisk, steady pace took me in and out of the long shadows in an almost hypnotic rhythm, and my awareness was drawn to the trees, to their energy and the life within them.

Then, in a moment, a strange thing happened. Had I known the term, I might have described it as an out-of-body experience. But I was not just out of my body: I was *within* something else. It was as if some part of me had become joined with the energy of the trees; then it seemed to be stretched out to join with other living things, at first plants, then further afield, until I felt I was touching a tremendous variety of life forms, both plant and animal.

In these brief moments I sensed an awareness of life as a whole unit, of a connection between all aspects of living energy. I was also aware of the way in which everything was constantly changing form as each being lived and died, returning to the energy of the whole. I understood life and death as a constant cycle, and that individuals are never completely separate from the whole. I experienced my whole lifetime as though it were a single picture, and realised the sense of continuity, of lives after lives.

I understood that there was no need for fear, no need to feel alone. At the same time I felt insignificant but not without value, for I was integral with that energy that was the whole of life. This realisation left me both comforted and exhilarated. My worries no longer seemed important. No longer did I feel like an isolated individual: I knew that I was a small part of something much greater, within which we were all connected.

Afterwards I tried to assess the event and to understand its essence in a logical way. Although I felt that I understood what had happened, it raised many questions for me. Because I had past-life memories the notion that we continue was not new to me. But at the age of sixteen I had never considered life as a single unit of energy, and I wondered about this experience of wholeness. For many years I read and studied whatever I could that related to this concept. This included the psychology of Carl Jung, who created the term 'collective unconscious', which I felt was a good way of expressing our connection with the energy of which we are a part. Later I came across the theory of Gaia, put forward by the distinguished British chemist James Lovelock and named after the Greek goddess of the Earth. It describes the world as a living, self-regulating unit of which we are a small and possibly dispensable part, and that all living things on this planet are connected and interdependent.

Although I have been through some difficult times since then, the sense of the connectedness of all beings has never left me. It underlies my view of life and of reincarnation. For me, the phrase 'everything is connected' is much more than a philosophy: it is a lived experience.

After passing my A-levels I spent three years training in London as a state-registered chiropodist, which would qualify me for a secure career. During this period I lost contact with several good friends who had gone on to university. Commuting to London each day while studying hard also took its toll, and although I did well in the exams I became extremely tired and quite severely depressed.

What I had not taken into account were my problems in relating to other people. I had become generally more socially confident, but my relationships with men were fraught with difficulties. During my college years I moved from one mismatch to another, unable to understand myself, let alone the structure of a good relationship. Some of this was undoubtedly due to my childhood fears of my father, but I wondered too how much it was related to my past lives. I knew that Mary had liked her father, but why was it so hard to remember her husband?

During that time I made efforts to explore Mary's marriage. It was easy to recall the early days. A good-looking, impressive man who seemed to appear on the scene just after the First World War, her husband was something of an outsider – Irish, but from another area. I was sure he had been a soldier. He seemed to have had several jobs at first, but mainly he had something to do with large timbers and roof work, a very skilled job in which he took pride. A quiet man, unable to discuss his feelings, he was at first the centre of Mary's life but later he seemed to be at home less and less. He did not even seem present in her thoughts for the children's future in those awful dreams of dying. I wondered whether clearer memories of him might have helped me understand my fear of close relationships and the difficulties and confusions they entailed.

These reached their peak when, towards the end of my second year at college, I entered into a relatively brief but disastrous relationship reminiscent of my early experiences as a victim of bullying. It revived and reinforced the fears that survived both from my childhood and from my memories of Mary.

While this relationship was at its worst, I was for some time disturbed by a psychic image that has appeared frequently at times of stress in my life. What I saw – reflected in mirrors, then superimposed on other faces and even posters – was my own face, no longer young but old and white-haired, looking back at me across time. It troubled me, though now I understand that this image was actually sent as a reassurance, as though my future self were trying to give me some comfort.

I needed to find someone I could discuss it with. Soon after the awful relationship was over, my mother came across a psychic who was highly recommended by a friend, and I went to see her. Her name was Mary; she was a gentle and very normal lady, separated from her husband and the mother of a teenage son. After I had told her something about myself she gave me a ring to hold. Instantly, I started seeing vivid mental pictures. I saw my hostess walking a dog by a river – a black dog with longish curly hair. Then I saw a Dutch house where I knew her friends lived, by what looked like a river, and then her ex-husband, standing apart from a group of people and brooding.

Mary asked me if the ring was warm; although I hadn't noticed it, it had actually become quite hot. She told me that the warmth of the ring was an indication that I was psychic; my ability to 'see' so easily was a bonus. She showed me a photograph of the dog – identical to the one I had seen – and told me she had Dutch friends who lived by a canal. She explained that this ability to see accurate images by holding an object was called psychometry.

Mary then went on to 'see' for me, and we discussed the vision of myself that had been troubling me. It was very reassuring to meet someone who had experiences like mine. As for the psychometry, it had never occurred to me that I could tap psychic information on purpose – this was fun!

After that, I would practise it for friends whenever the opportunity arose. The results varied, but quite often I could see detailed pictures of the past, present and, more rarely, the future. I was usually given objects like rings or keys, but my favourite items were antiques, especially weapons or tools that had been handled frequently, with concentration. When handling old items I experience a falling sensation, which took me by surprise the first few times it happened. I have found that the older the object the longer the 'falling time', so the sensation gives me an idea of its age. Sometimes I have seen pictures of the previous owner of, for example, an antique sword.

After qualifying in 1974, I worked briefly near Croydon in Surrey, where I met Steve, my husband-to-be. Steve was different; I felt comfortable and at ease with him from the first. We also had a strong intellectual connection that I had not found in other relationships, and Steve had a keen wit that I still appreciate.

Before a year had passed we found our home in North-amptonshire, a small but enchanting cottage by open fields, in a hamlet of about a dozen houses south of a small rural town. Alongside the demands of ordinary life, marriage and eventually two children, psychic experiences continued to occur frequently. Sometimes I had unlooked-for insights about my patients, and in my early married life I continued to practise psychometry from time to time, often giving people accurate and sometimes useful information.

I was happy with Steve; in marriage I no longer felt alone. As I learned how to share my life, I also learned through my work to understand people better, and I became more relaxed. The incursions from my past lives were less frequent as new experiences kept me occupied. From time to time, though, fragments of memory would emerge, and because I was happy it seems that Mary's memories at that time were the happier ones. Sometimes they were triggered by a smell or sound. The dry dusty smells of the harvest remind me of sitting outside Mary's cottage stuffing a mattress with straw, and the laughter as the children and I struggled to get the overlarge mattress through the doorway. The smells of straw, sawdust and creosote would immediately take me back to a small bedroom with a window divided into a number of panes. The smells seemed to be associated with the husband's working clothes.

When my son was born in 1979 I felt like a whole new person. With my need for security and financial independence I did not give up work entirely; but I gave priority to my need to be a mother. In motherhood and family life I began to find myself. I also grew closer to understanding some of the emotions relating to my memories, particularly

Mary's feeling of guilt. With a real child whom I could hold close, I could appreciate the power of Mary's emotion about leaving the children when she died. I could not leave my son even for a few hours, let alone bear the thought of total separation. I knew that I would see my children grow, and was confident in my husband's ability to look after them, but I wondered whether Mary lacked that confidence. I could never quite reach past the barriers of her guilt and distress, but something felt very uncomfortable.

★ ★ ★

I still had visions and flashes both of my past lives and of future events. One future vision, which – perhaps surprisingly – bothered me very little, happened in my late twenties when I foresaw my own death as an old woman. Although there was sadness at leaving my family, there was no sense of fear, and none of the suffering and guilt that made Mary's departure so painful.

The most consistent spontaneous psychic occurrence was telepathy – which for me is a reminder that we are all connected at some level. One day, while visiting a friend, I was hit by an emotional shockwave, which came from outside myself. I knew something was terribly wrong with a family member, and hurried home. I was relieved when Steve arrived back safely, but when I telephoned my mother she immediately told me that my younger brother had moved out of his increasingly difficult marriage and was in a very emotional state. From then on I realised that my link with Alan was such that it explained many past, though usually less strong, psychic surges I had experienced in connection with him.

In 1986 my brother Michael was fatally injured in a gliding accident. Alan was telephoned first and had the added worry of trying to locate the rest of us. At the exact moment when he received the call, my family and I were in a service station on the M1, and I was about to sit down with a cup of coffee. Suddenly the whole room seemed to spin and I fell into a seat, spilling some coffee. I was shaking and felt like crying; I told Steve something terrible had happened, but it was not until we got home that we learned of Michael's death. It was sad that our views and beliefs had clashed, for I had always hoped that we would be able to recover our former closeness.

I later discovered a similar link with my son. Because of Mary's memories, I never liked leaving my children alone. However, when my son was a teenager I had no problem about going on several one-day courses in podiatry (the new name for chiropody); he had his own front-door key. During the afternoon of the second course I suddenly became mentally aware of him, and I knew immediately that he had forgotten his key. I wondered whether he would go on to his casual and rather mucky job of egg collection at the nearby farm without changing out of his school clothes.

I turned to the person next to me and said, 'My son's forgotten his key!' I noted the time, and after a few seconds my anxiety disappeared. It transpired that he had forgotten his key, but rather than wear his school clothes in the chicken house he had sensibly taken some shorts and a T-shirt from the washing line.

With some people whom I know well I can recognise a 'signature', and know that a friend is writing me a letter or about to phone – this latter is of course a common experience with people who don't necessarily consider themselves psychic. However, one of my most powerful telepathic experiences concerned people with whom I had no connection, and I still have no idea why it happened. At the time of the Falklands War in 1982 I had been practising the Japanese martial art of aikido for about a year, and had found the techniques more effective when I entered a light, meditative yet focused state of mind – the same frame of mind as I used in psychic practice.

I was halfway through a particular throw when I suddenly became very dizzy and had to sit down. I felt that I was in a ship, trapped in a small corridor with about four men. It looked rather like the interior of a submarine and felt horribly claustrophobic. The ship was on fire and the doors at each end were sealed; the men were trapped. For about fifteen minutes I was sharing the last moments of these men, and they were terrified. The fear left me when I felt them die, but the shock remained with me for a considerable time.

Several people asked me if I was all right and I told them what I had seen and felt. Next day it was reported in the news that HMS *Sheffield* had been sunk by enemy fire the previous evening.

In 1979, Steve started a haulage business, which went well for a time. He was careful while the business was building up and I was working part-time, so we could just manage financially. The first indication of a problem was in 1982, when I tried to look at our future, using cards as a focus for my intuition. To my dismay I kept seeing things going wrong – a financial crisis and terrible emotional strain. At the time I didn't connect it with the vivid dream of disaster that had worried me at the age of sixteen. By 1983 – the year our daughter was born – the start of the recession was hitting the building industry, and one of the first casualties was haulage. In addition, the health authority I worked for cut back on part-time hours; I looked for private clients, but my practice was slow to build up. The next two or three years were incredibly difficult and stressful, and I became quite ill. Steve eventually had to give up his business.

During these years there came a day when I found myself arriving by car at the place of my dream. Although I knew that this heralded a number of severe crises – which turned out to be family- and health-related – it was something of a relief to know that that point had arrived. I also knew that once the crises had passed, our lives would ultimately improve. What I did not yet know was that this improvement would be connected with my discovery of Mary's lost family, and resolving the anguish that had remained with me from that past life.

From about 1980 onwards, as my children grew and my maternal feelings strengthened, so grew the need to trace the children I felt I had deserted. Those children had been deprived at an early age of what my own children were enjoying, and I had to do something about it. This need intensified as I approached my early thirties, the age of Mary's death.

Over the years, I had been making notes about my memories and seeking out maps of Ireland to see if I could get a clearer picture of Malahide, Mary's home, that would correspond to the maps I had drawn in childhood. In 1980 the Towcester Bookshop opened near our home, and one day I ordered a map showing the Malahide area at a scale of a quarter of an inch to the mile – at least it would be better than the school atlas. I explained to Peter Gooding, who

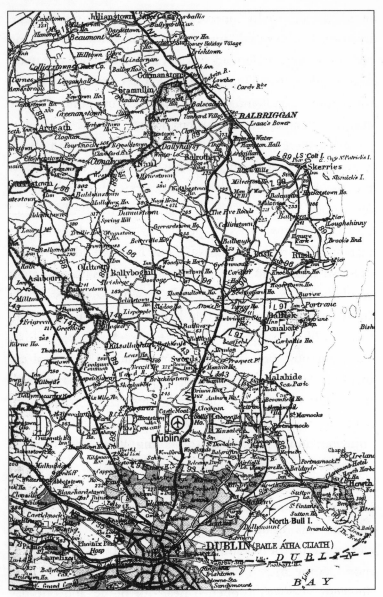

Section of map ordered from Towcester bookshop in 1980
(© Bartholomew. Reproduced with permission.)

owned the shop, why I wanted the map. If he thought me a little odd, he did not show it.

Mr Gooding telephoned me when the map arrived and I took my own sketch map with me to the shop for comparison. All the roads I had marked appeared on the new map, and the distances between them were fairly well to scale. The station was where I had placed it, and the road I had marked 'to the City' was the Dublin road. This was my first real confirmation that my dreams and memories were real. It was exactly the spur I needed to begin my search for Mary's family.

I still had very little to go on. I did not even know Mary's surname; without it I could do little at a distance, but, given our financial struggles, I could not afford to go to Malahide. I talked about it all endlessly with Steve, my mother and close friends, and their support and acceptance was invaluable. I had many discussions, too, with a local vicar, who was quite able to accept that there was more to life than the everyday. He too had a number of stories of unexplained happenings that he was keen on exploring in an unbiased way.

I also met other people who shared my psychic interests. Important among them was Mr Coulter, a retired man originally from the Republic of Ireland, who was very well read. It was while I was talking to him that the subject of reincarnation first came up seriously as a possible explanation for my memories. At first, in the interests of exploring every avenue, he wondered if I had some sort of genetic relationship with Mary's family, but I had no ancestors who would fit this particular bill.

Eventually, it was the strength of the emotions that I experienced as Mary that convinced Mr Coulter that her life had been real, and that I was remembering my previous life through reincarnation. We had many long discussions about aspects of reincarnation and books written on the subject. One interesting theory put forward by the past-life researcher Dr Ian Stevenson was that many children had spontaneous memories of remembered recent lives that had ended prematurely, through violence or illness. Dr Stevenson suggested that their 'souls' may have felt incomplete and reincarnated swiftly to complete unfinished business.

To me this sense of unfinished business rang true as a possible explanation of the urgency of Mary's memories, their remarkable consistency, and the tenacity with which they had remained in my consciousness. Mary's guilt at leaving her children did imbue my being and my emotions with a strong sense of a task unfinished. The sense of fear that accompanied this was less easy to explain. However, for Mary's sake, as well as my own, I knew that I must take the investigation further and find her children.

CHAPTER 3

Hypnosis

It has often happened in my life that a stroke of fate has enabled me to move forward. At times, circumstances and the helpfulness of others have paved the way for me to be swept along in a chain of events. For example, there was a window in time between 1985 and the early 1990s during which it was possible for me not only to research Mary's life, but to succeed in my research. One major reason was that I suddenly had time on my hands. Around 1987, when I was thirty-four, virtually all my close friends had either moved away or died. Steve had had to cut his business losses and for a while was working long hours, including weekends, doing agency driving work to bridge the gap while he built up a new business.

Steve and I had both been practising aikido for around seven years – I thought that was probably the closest I would ever get to the Japanese aspect of my makeup – but it became impossible for me to take the courses that would enable me to progress further. Steve was offered a class to teach at a youth centre fourteen miles away; I encouraged this, but it meant that I had to give up aikido, as it clashed with my own training night. So I had almost too much time alone to think and reflect and work towards resolving the past.

At the same time, however, I had been making contacts with helpful people such as Mr Coulter, and Peter Harris, who owned an antique-cum-junk shop in Towcester. Around 1981 I had got into the habit of dropping into the shop, not just to look for bargains, but to use psychometry to look into the history of some of the objects. A friendly, middle-aged man, Peter was someone I could share my experiences with, and we had some interesting times exploring both antique items and the history of his cottage.

Then I was introduced to June, a schoolteacher who was researching psychic phenomena for a thesis. An aikido instructor's wife suggested me to her as a possible subject, and I volunteered to take part in her research. This involved being connected to an electroencephalograph, which recorded the electrical activity in my brain during normal consciousness and then during psychic activity.

For the psychic part of the test I used psychometry: I concentrated on a watch belonging to the technician, and, while I described to her the images I saw, the graph recorded an extremely intense level of brain activity. After a few minutes the technician asked me to stop: the personal details I was giving her were making her feel uncomfortable – though she agreed that they were accurate.

For me this was another step towards a wider acceptance of my experiences, and it also had an important spin-off. Through the teacher I was introduced to Jim Alexander, a hypnotist who was researching the phenomenon of previous lives through regression. I attended one of his demonstrations in late 1987, but had no wish to be hypnotised in public. However, on 6 January 1988 he held a small meeting in a private house for a women's group, and this time I allowed myself to be hypnotised in front of the dozen or so people present.

Under hypnosis I described the cobbled street with the market stalls, and the familiar and painful scene of Mary's last moments – the memory I had never been able to escape from, that usually came to me when I was alone at night. Going through it again, I found tears uncontrollably rolling down my face. Normally I would never let myself cry in public, but the hypnosis took me to a level of mind where I seemed unable to apply normal constraints.

As a result of this, Jim offered me a course of hypnotic regression, to start on 10 February, which would be tape-recorded and documented; it would also be free. I accepted. I felt it was just what I needed to substantiate many of the memories I already had, and possibly learn more about Mary and her life. I might even discover her surname; this had always eluded me, presenting a major obstacle to my own research.

I was the first person Jim had worked with who had had past-life memories prior to hypnosis. A room in his home had been fitted with recording equipment and a large, comfortable chair in which I could relax. Here I sat some-what uneasily: I knew the process would feel invasive, but my need to find out more was greater than my instinct for privacy.

Jim asked me if on the previous occasion he had left a trigger, a subconscious command that would help him put me under more quickly. He had, though I was not sure whether it would work after a lapse of a month. The trigger was a touch on my shoulder, and it worked so fast that I hardly managed to finish my sentence before slipping into the strange slumber of the hypnotic state. There was a sensation of falling, followed by a little resistance, and then at last I sank into a deep chasm of semiconsciousness.

First of all, Jim asked me to remember a time in my early childhood, and these memories were not too uncomfortable: I was asked to describe my first day at school and the person I sat next to on the bus. Stage by stage, Jim took me further back until he asked me to return to a time before I was born.

I found myself recognisably as Mary, but I was not in the cottage at Malahide that I had expected to see. This was a young Mary, before marriage and children, and it was my first conscious recollection of this time. I was aware that Jim was asking questions, and I was also aware of listening to the answers. It was a little while before I realised that it was my own voice answering. It was as though I were two people: a spectator in the present, and Mary herself in a past that was very real. I could smell the grass on the slopes outside a large farmhouse, and I breathed in the fresh spring air. I felt that this was where I worked for a family called Lett.

Jim asked me how I was dressed. Looking down at my clothes, I heard my dissociated voice answering, 'A long, dark, wool skirt and an apron. The apron's not so long but the skirt nearly reaches the ground.' Then, inside the farmhouse, which seemed very familiar, I saw Mary cleaning the grate and laying a fire.

Someone said, 'Nineteen fifteen.' I realised that it was my voice – Jim must have asked what year it was, and Mary had answered. I was drifting between my two selves. Asked my age, I hesitated a little, and then, 'Seventeen.' As the questions and answers continued in this strange way, I seemed able to wander through the places I saw – they were vivid and tangible. I could feel the wind in my hair as though I were truly there.

I walked briskly down the hill from the house to the village where my family lived. It was north of Dublin, and I felt it was close to Malahide. There was a small stone house standing on its own, and thoughts of Mary's father and brothers came to me. Jim asked for names, but all I could come up with was a street called something like 'Walldown Lane'. I also saw a smithy and a shop; asked what it sold, I found my mind focusing on ribbons and the fact that it often ran out of bread.

Jim asked me to see 1919. Now Mary was walking down a main street with a postbox on the corner. I described her clothes: a handmade, calf-length skirt with an overlaid scalloped border and an underlayer in contrasting fabric. I felt pride in the needlework. Beside Mary was her husband, a smartly dressed man of perhaps twenty-five, and the centre of Mary's attention. He seemed a little distant, possibly arrogant, and, as Mary looked at him, he turned round to see if he was being noticed by anyone else.

Jim asked me to describe what I could see. I realised it was Malahide; I was in the main north-to-south road in the middle of the village. Pressed for the husband's name I hesitated, and uncertainly said, 'Bryan.' It was a name I had used in childhood games. Asked about his job, I described the large timbers up high and some other jobs before he 'went back' – back where, I didn't know. Jim had some queries relating to the First World War, but, although I had always thought of Mary's husband as a soldier, my response seemed clouded. I may have been trying too hard to produce the right answers.

During the next part of the session I felt confused about places and events. Asked about a church that I knew to be on a road where I felt there was also a butcher's, I found the outside easy to describe but not the interior, suggesting that it was not Mary's usual church. There was a large gable end close to the road, with coping stones along the top and a pier at each side with a stone on top. I saw a small wedding taking place in this church, but did not feel it was Mary's. Instructed to look in the register and give a name and a date, I offered these with unlikely clarity. The name I gave was O'Neil and the date 1921, but I was not at all sure these were correct.

Later I saw Mary's home, the one I usually remembered. It was a fairly traditional cottage, first on the left on the straight, dusty lane that ran west from the south end of Malahide. Other details seemed consistent with my previous dreams and memories. Taken further forward in time, I described a small girl with a mop of darkish hair. I gave her date of birth as 4 February 1922, but, although this felt right as a rough date, I doubted its exactness.

Too soon, I was being woken. At first I could hardly move, but, after a few moments, full consciousness and mobility returned. What had felt like only ten minutes had actually taken an hour.

When I got home that evening I made rapid notes, hoping there might be even one piece of useful information. The names O'Neil and Bryan didn't seem quite right, but I had ventured further back into Mary's life than ever before, and had seen many new things. I marked the position of the butcher's and the church on one of my maps so that they might one day be checked; I even noted the dates about which I was so dubious. I desperately needed to find a key to start my search, and anything might turn out to be that key.

Two weeks later I had my second session of hypnosis. This time Jim was interested in looking at the time between the 1930s, when Mary died, and my own birth in 1953. This was more relevant to Jim's research than to mine, but I was still interested. It could even be useful in understanding or proving the continuity of the soul, which is one of the major concepts in most theories about reincarnation.

This time, when I was touched on the shoulder, I was instructed to go Mary's final memories. Once again I endured the physical pain and anguish that, in some perverse way, I almost needed to experience, as though their very familiarity would refuel my determination.

It was autumn when Mary died. My viewpoint drifted to a point above and a little to one side of her thin, now vacant body. The room was white and empty; she had died alone in what looked like a hospital. I cannot say how much time passed before someone entered the room and sat hunched over by the bed; I thought it must be Mary's husband, but this man seemed somehow gentler, his feelings more open. Then I felt myself drift further away into a very calm darkness. Time itself ceased to be definable; everything felt as though in suspended animation.

Somewhere in the blackness, as Jim's voice talked me through the years, a small memory emerged. As we came to 1940 there was a subtle change of awareness that I can only describe as a need to 'be something' again. By 1945 I was aware of being a small child. Nothing was very clear, but there was a feeling of being alone, or simply lonely. And there was noise, confusion and untidiness.

Jim drew me back in time again to Ireland. I saw a growing

family, and felt Mary become less entranced with the joys of parenthood now that there was a houseful of children. My brief descriptions of several of the children were consistent with previous memories, and I also mentioned a baby boy who died at birth.

I heard Jim's voice directing me again to drift much further back – several hundred years. By chance I found myself in one of the memories that had been with me since child-hood, although I did not at first recognise it. I seemed to stop, suddenly petrified. It was 1716. For several minutes I described the fears of a seven-year-old French country girl – Anna, apparently – who had been sold into service to a household in Boulogne. I saw images of a large family, a journey with her father and a farmhouse left behind, and felt the terror of never seeing her family again. As if the trauma of Mary's memories were not enough, this trauma was now left in my conscious mind, with its familiar feelings of injus-tice and anger mingled with fear.

Too soon, Jim's voice drew me back to the present and I was left with shreds of memory, some tantalising, some terrifying . . .

★   ★   ★

As the weeks went by, the experience of hypnosis was becoming all-consuming. Doors left slightly ajar were now opening up so wide, and at such speed, that there was little time to come to terms with the significance of what was going on. The hypnosis was breaking down all the internal barriers that I had erected to protect myself. Although I had always remembered the pain, I had rationalised everything to enable me to carry on as myself. The intensity of recall under hypnosis left me feeling exposed, raw, vulnerable and confused. There was a tremendous conflict between self-preservation and the needs of the past. From a psychological point of view, it is often better to face things rather than repress them, but the trauma of doing so should not be underestimated.

It irritated me, too, that with hypnosis it was so easy to gain a level of recall and of detail that I was unable to reach by myself, even after years of practice. I was annoyed that it had taken so long to discover that this was possible, and wondered if I had wasted all those years. Time became my enemy. I wanted to know everything and find my family *now*. The two weeks between sessions were painful; it was like an addiction, and I did not want it to stop until I had all my answers. It never occurred to me that I might need this time and some more maturity before I was ready to go further forward.

At the next session, guided straight back to Mary, I spoke without being asked. 'My baby is dead.' I could see a woman, presumably a nurse, handing me the dead infant so that I could hold it and say goodbye. The grief at that loss is present still, each time the memory is brought to mind. I held the baby and understood. I felt thankful that it was possible to look at my baby and say goodbye. Had there been another time when Mary had not said goodbye?

The child was a boy. Mary already had several boys, and was now in her thirties. Jim asked if that was a good age to have children, and I replied that it was not unusual. But inside, as Mary, I felt angry at the stupid question – as if there was any choice about having children!

Jim took me back again. My mind obediently responding, I found myself sitting on a grassy slope. Before me was a panoramic view of rolling hills running down to a distant stretch of water. I could smell the earth and the growing plants. It was beautiful, and I wanted to be able to get up and walk over the hills for miles.

Jim was asking questions about work. Mary, now fifteen, did not want to think about work, stuck in that big house cleaning all day. It was much better to be out here. But she liked her employer, Mrs Lett. The house had a white pillar either side of the porch, but was a large farmhouse rather than a mansion. Mrs Lett would sit in the main room, which occupied the full depth of the right side of the house, with large windows front and back. She was fairly old and did not go out much.

The main room was wonderful, with a large carpet rich with warm reds and russets filling most of the floor. On the walls were framed mirrors and about the room stood chairs with arms and lots of other beautiful furniture – desks and tables, nothing large, everything elegant – including Mrs Lett with her pearl necklace and pale skin. There was a level of wealth here that was clearly outside Mary's usual experience.

I described the house as Jim took me through it. The kitchen was at the back, where there was also a small wash-room and utility rooms. The cook did not do the tiresome or dirty jobs, and it was Mary who did the cleaning, scrubbing and washing.

We went forward a little in time: now Mary was married with a family and was cleaning the cottage. Jim asked me about household tasks and what I was using to clean with.

Part of me understood why he asked these questions, but another part of me was of that time and felt irritated. My replies were sometimes curt: 'A damp cloth.' I could see a block of soap which was used to scrub the clothes before washing them. Then Jim asked me about dishes. The level of irritation rose as I described soap in small flakes that was used for dish-washing, knowing full well that there was none at home – it cost too much.

It was quiet; most of the children were at school. Jim asked about the school, but I could not see a name, just the letter C. I did not know if they used slates, but had seen a book that the eldest girl had written in. She was clever and hard-working, and I had great hopes for her – perhaps she could become a nurse. One of the older boys was difficult at times, and overenergetic.

Next, the instruction came to go back to France and Anna in Boulogne. Then we went forward again beyond Mary and, step by step, to the child between 1940 and 1945. It was a short memory of a short life but I came up with a lot of detail about the locality, including a possible street name. (My efforts at tracing this life are described in the Appendix.)

Then I was taken forward again, through the darkness, slowly, until there was a light ahead, at first just a spot. I wanted to go towards it. As I reached it there was a feeling of warmth, actual physical warmth and comfort, following a time of no physical awareness. There was now a sense of pure *being*.

As an observer, I found this hard to accept, yet at the time I seemed to understand what it was about. My conscious self knew that we had reached a point just before my own birth. Awareness and senses grew; then there was the feeling of being held tightly, followed by light and noise and people.

My head emerged facing left and then turned upwards. There was noise and confusion, followed by the need to be held as closely confined as before, for both comfort and security. Soon that need was being fulfilled, but too quickly I was being taken away, and I did not want to go. I was not being held firmly, and I was neither secure nor where I had wanted to stay.

I observed all this with some incredulity, before Jim spoke again and drew my mind back to the present. He tried to calm my remaining anxiety. Perhaps aware of the guilt that Mary's death caused me, he told me that unfinished tasks from the past should be left. But this was contrary to my lifetime's habit of not leaving the past – or, it would be truer to say, *it* would not leave *me*, nor could it.

I checked later with my mother and found that I had 'seen' my birth fairly accurately – she particularly remembered my head turning up. As to my being taken away, it was the midwife's first delivery and she was so delighted that I was such a large and mature-looking baby that she showed me off all round the hospital before I was returned to my mother. I wonder if this has anything to do with my aversion to crowds of people and noise, and being in the limelight.

The project was beginning to affect my daily life; it was never out of my mind. At times the depth of emotion attached to the visions of the past was unbearable. Memories were also rising up between sessions, adding to the information that needed to be assessed and understood. I became immensely frustrated, mainly because everything seemed to be moving too slowly. Jim himself was slow and methodical, which was probably necessary to his task. I felt like a child waiting for Christmas, with no idea when Christmas would come.

On my next visit, Jim was still interested in looking at many different times, and our first excursion was to Wales in the Dark Ages, a thousand years ago. Then he took me back to find Mary, but there was so much jumping about in time that it was hard to remember it all afterwards. The intention was to check dates, names and events for continuity. I did remember a telephone number given as that for the Letts' house – 71 34 with a prefix, possibly 61. This was useful, as it could be checked. (Later, I discovered that Irish telephone numbers are made up of six digits in three pairs, as I had given them, and the number would be viable for the areas where I expected the farmhouse to be, near Dublin.)

I saw a doctor who visited Mrs Lett, partly as a friend; he wore a long dark coat and a hat with a dent in the crown. He drove about the only car I had seen; it was black and shiny, with huge wheel arches. Inside the main room of the house there were books; Jim asked me about their titles but I did not answer. I could see one by Tolstoy and other classics, but my present self was unable to accept that such detail could be accurate. Confused, I said too little, yet I could see the whole room in perfect detail.

The farmhouse itself was set high on a hill with extensive views, especially to the back. I also seem to remember taking an interest in someone upon the roof of one of the outbuildings – may this have been the young man who became Mary's husband?

* * *

The accuracy of a past-life memory gained through hypnosis may not be 100 per cent perfect – it is like any other memory of the past, which may well be flawed. However, it is the emotional content of our memories that affects us the most strongly. This is why hypnotic regression can be a useful form of therapy to help people come to terms with unresolved feelings. Often, traumatic past events – whether in this or previous lives – inhibit us from living a full life, although we may not remember the events themselves.

In my case, hypnosis helped me to resolve my feelings in one instance by enabling me to look more deeply into my memory of Anna, the French servant girl. Her life had been with me since childhood, but an important part of it had always eluded me. Before hypnosis, I had mainly recalled her adolescence and early adulthood, which were lightened by the friendship of a fellow servant girl. Although we worked hard, we enjoyed laughing and giggling as we scrubbed or dusted. However, I very much disliked remembering Anna's sense of being clumsy and unattractive. I was painfully aware of her lack of education; remembering her illiteracy would make me cringe with embarrassment.

It was only under hypnosis that I relived the terrible day when my parents sold me into service. Recovering this painful memory, even though the emotion was shattering, helped me to understand why recalling this particular life made me feel so unloved and unwanted. Hypnosis also cast light on the later part of Anna's life, which was spent moving from town to town trying to find casual work, depressed by the widespread squalor and poverty. I remember her life only as far as about the age of fifty; Anna seems never to have married and became increasingly isolated emotionally.

Later I was able to put this life into historical context: it was in the years running up to the French Revolution, when social conditions were very bad. Now I could understand why I had been sold as a child: my parents had loved me, but had had no other choice. I was able to come to terms with the hardship of my later life, and to release myself from the feeling that all the difficulties had somehow been my fault.

The life before Anna, again found under hypnosis, was difficult to remember. I was a young boy in 1650, and there was something wrong with me: there was a kind of space between myself and others that suggested either deafness or autism. I couldn't talk or understand speech. I saw the workshop where my father cut timber; several men worked here but my father, a kind and tolerant man, was the one person I trusted. Since it was impossible to speak at the time, Jim had no way of knowing that I was seeing anything.

As we jumped about through the centuries I had one very brief glimpse of a time as a small boy in a large Tudor house, with floors covered in huge, cold stone slabs and wall hangings that helped cut out the draughts. Even further back, on a date I gave as 1223, there was Gwen, the dumpy eighteen-year-old daughter of a family who, though not rich, were financially secure. I was at a gathering to welcome home my brothers, who had been away at the Crusades. (Checking the date afterwards, I found it was consistent with the *later* Crusades.) I saw a huge, solid wooden table on which was laid a variety of pies, bread, nuts and berries, suggesting an autumn feast. This felt like a good time – very simple, but happy.

Before Gwen, I recalled being Effan in Wales; asked what year it was, I said it was during the reign of Dafydd (which may have been around AD 800). As Effan, I had a family of young children by the age of twenty. This life seemed very happy, despite problems typical of the time: two of my children seem to have died of an illness, possibly a virus like the smallpox, which had struck the whole village, taking a number of children.

I described the village, a collection of rectangular buildings on wooden frames, probably covered with wattle and daub. On the day I was reliving it, it had rained so heavily that the track out of the village was waterlogged and a cart was stuck in the mud. It was blocking the way, while the villagers discussed what to do about it. I was aware of my body as Effan: I was slight in build and wore a dull-coloured, shapeless garment woven of coarse wool. It was scratchy but warm; later I found out that this weave was called homespun, which would have been worn at that time.

It was during this session that Jim decided to test my psychic sense. I was still under hypnosis when he brought me back to the present, but without waking me. He asked me to 'move up' towards the ceiling and stop above a small cupboard. When I saw the cupboard as if from above, he told me that he had put something there and asked me to describe it. On the cupboard top I saw two flattish square shapes the size of gramophone records, and a long cardboard or paper tube stretching the length of the top.

Jim woke me and I struggled back to consciousness. He had put a coin in a box, hoping I would find it, but I had not picked up on such fine detail. The square shapes were in fact two record decks, and the tube was a rolled-up poster, which he had forgotten was there. As a test of clairvoyance under hypnosis, this was merely interesting. But as a test of the accuracy of the information that I was giving it was quite valuable, confirming my ability to give broad outlines and pictures that lacked fine detail. I felt this could apply to the regression as well: I could 'see' Mary, her children, the cottage and the village, but I could not 'see' with precise accuracy the names of people and roads, nor dates. Although I was quite sure that the name Mary was correct, I still did not know her surname, nor that of her parents.

There were two important past-life memories that we never touched on during hypnosis sessions – perhaps because Jim was very much in charge of where and when we travelled to in memory. One was my Japanese life, which came immediately before Mary's (I describe it more fully in Chapter 9). The other was my happiest memory of all, which had been with me from childhood.

I was a young man and had been away from my village for a long time, probably hunting. My main image is of walking over the last hill before reaching home, and seeing the collection of small round huts clustered by the shore of a great lake. I was alone and returning with a great sense of triumph. The land around was very green and the weather mild. Beyond the lake I could see mountains to the right, and to the left a forest that would take uncountable days to cross, if it could be crossed at all. There were no obvious signs of cultivation; most of the land seemed to be forested.

My clothing was of animal hide, but it was soft and supple, carefully stitched. I carried all that I needed for survival and valued each small possession in an almost mystical way. In my present life I tend to surround myself with clutter; the simplicity of my possessions in that earlier life gave me a great sense of freedom.

This snatch of time may have been pre-Celtic. The Celts, who were farmers and weavers, arrived in Britain about 600 BC. The image I recall is of a far more primitive time, with apparently no woven cloth or land cultivation, although some land had been cleared of trees. Farming actually began in Britain during the New Stone Age, around 3500 BC. The village I saw consisted of no more than a handful of round huts, probably built of wood, with thatched roofs, which could place it as early as 3000 BC. I am uncertain about the country, but it was somewhere with a temperate climate – possibly a settlement in Scotland during the late Stone Age. But most important to me is that it was a moment of tremendous joy. This is the image that has come to me in dreams and at other times, whenever I feel a sense of achievement or fulfilment.

CHAPTER 4
On the Trail

Although it was fascinating to look back through other times and places, the roller-coaster ride through time that Jim took me on was achieving little towards my own quest. But, though I still had insufficient information, it did not occur to me that it was too soon to forge ahead. I felt unable to control the extremes of emotion bubbling up and taking over so much of my time.

I was given an extra impetus by a gift from Mr Coulter. I had been talking obsessively to him and other friends between these sessions, and bemoaning the lack of verifiable detail in so many areas. After one of his trips to Ireland, he brought me an Ordnance Survey map of the Dublin area, at one inch to the mile – far more detailed that any map I'd consulted so far. Not only were the station and churches where I had placed them, either originally or after hypnosis, but the road conformations were even more clearly those I had drawn as a child. Names suddenly leaped at me – 'Gay Brook' in particular meant something to me, though I was not sure what – but, most importantly of all, I saw the line of the stream that I had always known ran near to Mary's cottage. I could hardly contain my excitement.

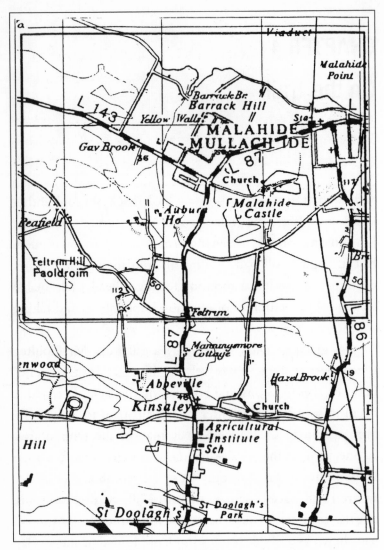

Malahide in Ordnance Survey map, 1988

With two more hypnosis sessions to go, and the Ordnance Survey map to hand, I felt a great urge to check any details I could. I wondered about the name 'O'Neil', which had come up in one session; it seemed wildly unlikely that I would find a connection, but it was worth a try. At the local library I got out the Dublin telephone directory, and noted several O'Neils who lived within a reasonable radius of Malahide. I started by writing to one. I enclosed a copy of the street map I had drawn, now with the identifying names of Malahide, Swords (the nearest town) and Gaybrook. I made the enquiry sound purely genealogical, reckoning that most people would find the real reason for it altogether too odd:

Please excuse the intrusion but I am trying to trace a family who lived fairly near to you. They may have had the same family name, and I wondered if there was any family connection.

The family I am searching for lived in the first cottage on the left on the road marked on the map enclosed. This was during the 1920s and 1930s. There were at least six or more children, and the mother, whose name I believe was Mary, died in the 1930s.

This first letter was the fruit of all my pent-up frustration. I had waited over thirty years before being able to do anything definite about tracing Mary. I had tried to be patient, but somewhere out there was the answer. Shortly afterwards I sent similar letters to other O'Neils in the area, and waited eagerly for their replies.

There was a feeling of unreality about it all. I was aware, as always, of the part of me that was Mary, but now she shared my mind in a new way. Memories of events in Mary's life began to find their way into my conscious mind on a daily basis, much as they had in my childhood. I spent a lot of time concentrating on the children's faces and refamiliarising myself with their personalities. Yet again I went through the torment of separation. Logic told me that the children had long since grown up and had lived their own lives for many decades, but I needed to know what had happened to them so that I could allow them to grow up in my own memory.

There were still many uncertainties. Hypnosis was revealing a lot I had not remembered spontaneously, but this new knowledge lacked the fine detail that I believed necessary for a successful search. I *saw* a great deal that I did not actually record in words, either because I was not asked about it or because Jim's questions were not relevant to what I was seeing. My own natural taciturnity may have played a part – I am sure the tapes must have contained many gaps and silences.

For instance, in one session I had a very clear picture of a trapped animal. The older boys, and perhaps one of the older girls, had set a snare. It was checked every day, and one morning they rushed in, talking about having caught something. All the children ran out to look, and I remember being last out because my hands were wet – I was still drying them on a cloth as I joined the group. It must have been a cool day, or fairly early, because my hands remained feeling damp and cool, as did the cloth on which I had dried them. I looked over the heads gathered round the snare and saw a hare. It was caught by the lower part of its body, so that it looked very long and thin. The trap had been set near a group of trees and undergrowth close to the cottage. I saw all this in my head, and recorded it later, but all that I said aloud at the time was, 'It's still alive!'

In Mary's parents' home there were memories of her father and two older brothers; I had no idea of their surname. I saw the Letts' house only under hypnosis. Then I saw Mary in about 1919 with her husband, possibly in Malahide. The idea that he was not a local man and probably fought in the First World War was present both in my memories and under hypnosis; so was the consciousness of his work involving timbers and being up high, and some basic details of his personality.

Every time I thought of him the memories were the same. They were clear at an early point, but were blotted out at a later stage, and I did not know why. When I saw the attractive, self-confident young man, I had feelings that were quite joyful. But later, after the children had arrived, Mary's happiness had changed, chiefly to a sense of quiet caution. The husband became surly and withdrawn, possibly disappointed with life, and was seldom at home.

The most consistent memory was of the cottage in Malahide. My descriptions of the children were consistent, too, although their numbers were not. Under hypnosis there seemed to be at least five, but I was sure there could have been as many as eight. Under hypnosis I named four of them – James, Mary, Harry and Kathy – but I felt as doubtful about these names as about their father's. This is one of the drawbacks of hypnotic regression: anxious to please the hypnotist, the subject may come up with invented answers rather than giving no reply. However, I was quite certain of the name Mary.

The two principal geographical areas of the memories seemed to be fairly close to each other and were both north of Dublin: one was the parents' home and the other was

Malahide. The general dates and timescale were so consistent that I felt they could be relied on. This meant that Mary's death occurred in the 1930s when she was in her mid-thirties.

Not many people have the chance to fulfil a dream, quite literally. Now that I had begun to take action, I was totally obsessed with my research. I was unable to stop thinking or talking about it, possibly to the irritation of other people. But I had a sense of being very much alive, living a new, exuberant reality. Untroubled as yet by a lack of replies from the various O'Neils, I began to rush about looking for possible enquiries to make.

I haunted the local library; it contained not only telephone directories for the whole of Ireland, but also reference books that gave useful addresses such as those of record offices. I found several Letts listed in the area, confirming that it was a local name, but there was still no guarantee that I had recalled the name correctly. I discovered that many files in the Dublin Record Office had been destroyed by fire during the uprising of 1922 – these may possibly have included some that would have been useful. However, I decided that it would make sense at this point to try to trace a more recent record, such as Mary's death certificate.

I also learned that records were held by priests, and this might be another avenue to explore. I therefore tried to identify the church I had seen under hypnosis, on the main road in Malahide, and found what I thought must be the right one in the telephone directory. I wrote a letter to the priest in charge, outlining the problem, as I had done to the O'Neils. Much later, the letter was returned, and I realised I had misread the address. By that time I was once again deep in uncertainties, primarily about Mary's surname, and felt that I might be clutching at straws. Deep down I knew that there was a strong chance that I was off-centre with the information I was using.

Finally, I investigated the cost of travel to Dublin, which would enable me to visit Malahide to ask about the family. Flying would be quickest and cause the least disruption to domestic life, but we were still struggling financially, and it was out of the question.

I knew that I must either find the family or try to forget them. To continue to remember without being able to find them would become unbearable. I reminded myself that there were well-documented studies of children whose previous life memories had been scientifically checked by Dr Ian Stevenson, and that in some cases their previous families had been found. But such cases tended to be produced with a view to proving reincarnation or at least providing convincing evidence. (It is impossible actually to prove migration of a soul from one life to another because we cannot scientifically identify the soul.) Nor did these case histories describe the feelings of the principals concerned, or how they coped with their memories.

Once again I began to consider why and how I had the memories, trying to rationalise the means by which they had become mine. One theory is that 'past-life memory' is a collection of ideas collated through reading history books, listening to others and so on, which are assembled under hypnosis into a kind of 'pseudo memory'. But as it happens, my own knowledge of and interest in history is embarrassingly poor, and my family had no connections with Malahide. Probably the most interesting confirmed detail to date was the statistically unlikely accuracy of my hand-drawn map, which could not have been produced from my imagination. The only theory that made sense to me is that such memories are definitely of previous lives and run in sequence because they are a continuation of the same essential soul, or person. However hard this is for some people to accept, if it is viewed logically without emotive rejection, it is viable.

I went over these arguments in my need to be certain, driven on by my gnawing concern over Mary's family. It had all taken too long: her children would be in their sixties or thereabouts, and would have come to terms with their past. I did not see that I could be of any value to them. Only the thought that perhaps the search had *had* to wait until this time could stem my feelings of failure. I was now about the same age as Mary at the time of her death. I had my own children and had experienced some quite severe problems in my life that might help me to understand a little better the family that was left behind. I remembered Mary as a worthy woman; perhaps now I could deem myself worthy enough to carry her memory with me.

★   ★   ★

At the next hypnosis session I was more self-critical, less detached. I was beginning to find the whole thing too traumatic. At the start, Jim directed me back to 1850 and asked me to describe what I saw. At first there was a ship with three sails. My voice mumbled as the scene opened out. My responses to Jim's questions were poor at first, which tended to be the case when the hypnosis was very deep. However, I managed to describe the life of a girl of about fifteen, named

Jane Matthews. Later, I spent some time researching her life; my search is described in the Appendix.

Jane lived with her large family in Southampton, very close to the west docks, in a small terraced house in a narrow street that ran slightly downhill into the main quayside road. There I could see large ships; one was very impressive with three tall masts. I mentioned a street name and details of the dockside to the west of the city. I described a flower seller, dock workers, sailors . . . My father in this life was a violent drunkard; most of his aggression was directed towards our work-worn mother, who took in washing and mending. I had a friend, a tall, thin boy around my own age. We would forage for extra food at the docks, mainly goods that fell out of damaged packages, fearful of being caught. If we found anything I would take my share home for my mother and siblings.

I remembered hiding with a younger sister when my father returned home drunk one evening, and witnessing a beating. I realised that before long it would be my turn, and soon after this I seem to have made a decision to leave home. It was a bad period in history to run away with nowhere to live: there was a risk of being arrested for vagrancy. It must have been spring, because I can remember eating hawthorn shoots plucked from hedgerows, while the nights were fairly cold. My final memory was of hiding in a stable, lying near a horse and feeling very weak and hungry. I have no memory of the exact moment of dying; everything seemed to merge – the smell and warmth of horses, the musty straw – into a strange, dissociated feeling in which I just drifted away.

One interesting detail was that the boy with whom I went scavenging reminded me very much of my present-life husband, Steve. When people are regressed it is not at all unusual for them to discover that people they know in their current lives have also featured in previous ones. This could explain that sense of 'instant recognition' people sometimes feel on first meeting an apparent stranger. Sometimes whole groups of people appear to reincarnate together.

★　★　★

Once again we returned to Mary, this time in 1922. Jim asked me many questions about a variety of things, some of which I would have been able to answer as my present self, yet could not answer as Mary. This was confusing and puzzling. For example, he asked me if there was any trouble, but as Mary I did not understand what he meant – there was always trouble somewhere! Then he asked me about the Letts, but I could tell him little; I thought they had moved away. Asked about the church where the children were baptised, I couldn't find its name. In response to a query about a priest, I had a name in my mind, Michael – but I later questioned this, as my older brother Michael had been a padre in the RAF.

Jim asked questions about the cottage. I told him that the name of the road it stood in began with the letter S, and it was rented from a man nicknamed 'Mac'. Instructed to go to the happiest memory of Mary's life, I immediately saw the birth of her first son. Jim went on asking questions that Mary thought silly, and there was a touch of impatience and sarcasm in her replies.

Struggling to wake again was hard, as always. There was much to discuss but at this point, Jim decided I should have a break from hypnosis for a couple of months. This was frustrating as far as my search was concerned, but at the same time something of a relief. Jim thought I should avoid becoming too wrapped up in the experience. I would have denied this at the time, but later I realised just how involved and affected I had been.

I could no longer cope with the lack of replies to my enquiries, and I decided to telephone the first O'Neil I had written to. It is not in my nature to push people and I felt rather uncomfortable, but in the event Mr O'Neil was quite interested and helpful.

'Oh, yes, we've been asking around and there was a family on the Dublin road it could have been,' he said.

'The Dublin road?' I replied. 'No, I'm pretty sure the family I'm looking for lives on the road to Swords, as on the map I sent.'

He said he couldn't quite place the roads on the map, but offered to do some searching. If he was going to go to some trouble for me, I felt duty-bound to be honest. So, when he asked about my connection to the family, I told him it was a little odd and hard to explain – that the map and other details had come from dreams I had had since childhood.

He went very quiet, then said, 'You're joking!'

Extremely embarrassed, I managed to explain that a few things, like the map, had turned out to be correct. I also told him about the baby boy who had died at birth. He listened patiently, but with obvious reservations. I should have antici-pated his reaction, but I started to feel a little paranoid. I hadn't heard from any other O'Neils; now I imagined all the people I had written to in the Malahide area comparing notes and deciding the whole thing was too bizarre to warrant any response.

However, a day or so later Mr O'Neil rang back. He had looked again at my hand-drawn map, checked it against a street map of Malahide, and found it to be more accurate than he expected – especially given that it had been drawn from dreams. He again offered to help, and I felt better about having been open with him.

I wrote straight off to the Irish Tourist Board asking for a Malahide street map, and soon I was looking at a very detailed map. Everything I knew about it sprang into greater prominence. As before the railway and churches were marked. The road with the church I had seen under hypnosis was actually called Church Road. The main road running east to west was The Mall, later becoming the Dublin Road which ran south to the city. The jetty onto the estuary was clearly visible and Gaybrook was just where the cottage had been. Best of all, I now had the name of Mary's road: Swords Road, leading to the village of Swords.

Now I could see how my whole approach to finding the family could change direction. I could go back to basics and try to trace the family who had lived in the first cottage on the left on Swords Road. If, when I found them, their family history seemed to fit, I could go on to see whether any of their personal memories matched mine. Unable to follow up this line of research in person, I had to work out how to ask for information at a distance, and whom to ask.

First I collated all the queries I had that could be answered, and compiled a kind of questionnaire, including information gleaned from the new street map, asking about the present or past existence of a cottage marked on the map, and whether anything could be found out about any family that might have lived there. I also asked for descriptions of the three churches in Malahide.

I hoped to find someone local who would be willing and able to find out the answers. I have never liked asking other people to do things for me, so I kept the list short and simple – I considered local history societies, the Rotary Club, women's groups and the local council, or perhaps I could find a volunteer. If I could get some sort of lead I could then take over and do the bulk of the work myself. While deciding whom to send the questionnaire to, I composed an advertisement for the Irish supplement to *Mensa Magazine* (I had belonged to Mensa since 1988). It read, 'Help needed in a limited amount of research of an unusual nature in the Malahide area.'

At last I felt I was getting somewhere. As my excitement grew, I became increasingly reluctant to be hypnotised again. As the next session was to be the last, I realised that Jim would want to see whether I would come up with the same answers as before, but I really didn't want to go through it all again. However, the arrangement had been made, and the break between sessions had allowed me to stand back a little and be realistic about the effects of the hypnosis.

Surprisingly, I found myself more relaxed than usual, though the session was confusing. Jim wanted to go back over dates and names, to test whether they were consistent, so there was a lot of changing about from place to place and time to time. Most of the names were the same, but there were enough changes to make me suspicious about the names in general. My main concern afterwards was that I might just be remembering what I had said before.

When it was all over I felt as though I had been left almost where I was before the hypnosis had started. I had a family to find, who lived at a specific location, and about whose personal history I had some details, but no surname that I could rely on. The search would still have to be based on the information I had had since childhood. At the same time, some of the details that came up during hypnosis helped to complete the picture, while several were very useful in confirming that I knew things about the family that no outsider could know. The hypnosis also played a large part in increasing my motivation and confidence.

I had still received no response to any of the other O'Neil letters, nor from the Dublin Records Office. I did, however, meet a friend of Mr Coulter's, Colin Skinner, a former history teacher who was studying theology in Dublin. He had a strong interest in Irish history, and expressed an interest in helping. I gave him a copy of the hand-drawn map, all the details I knew about the family and their home, and the questionnaire. I also gave him the description and a drawing of the church I had described under hypnosis; I still thought that this was where the family records might be held.

Mr Skinner asked if he might use my notes of the memories as part of a thesis, as they brought up a number of ideas of theological interest. I was happy for him to do this; I have always accepted that there are a variety of views on any situation. For him to look at the information and discuss it from his standpoint could only be to the good, even if it turned out that he was totally opposed to my beliefs. I also thought it was a good idea to share the research, since independent checking would leave less room for mistakes or misinterpretations. It was important to carry out the task properly.

Then I received an answer to the advertisement I had

placed in *Mensa Magazine*. It was from a freelance journalist who lived in Swords, the next town to Malahide; she wrote that, since she was constantly doing research, a little extra would be no problem. I replied, enclosing my questionnaire and adding:

Before I can ask you to do anything, to be fair, I must explain why the research is unusual because you may feel that you would rather not be involved. This is 'past-life memory research', however that may be interpreted. If you do want to help I would willingly explain myself further should you wish.

I never heard from her again.

★   ★   ★

Time passed, I was making very little progress and there was scant feedback from the new contacts – nothing at all from any of those I had written to. What I really needed was to make contact with someone who had lived in Malahide for a number of years and could remember the families living there in the 1920s and 1930s. Ideally, I needed to go there myself, but our finances ruled this out.

Despite my initial optimism, as the end of 1988 approached I began to slow down. My burst of hyperactivity – as well as the stress of the hypnosis – had worn me out. My metabolism swung into a weary lower gear, and as winter began I entered an almost hibernatory state. I knew that I could do little until I got over my depression. This was the worst I had felt for many years, and in the end I had to resort to medication, for the first time in my life. I had reached my lowest ebb.

CHAPTER 5

Discoveries

Just as I was beginning to despair, fate stepped in once more. I was still working part-time for the health authority, but needed to expand my private practice to increase my income. In January 1989, completely out of the blue, I was offered a quite a lot of work from a state-registered chiropodist who was moving away. Suddenly I had the chance to move forward. Over the next couple of months, as my depression slowly lifted and my earnings grew, it became clear that I would at last be able to visit Malahide. I discussed it with Steve, and planned the trip for the first weekend in June. I booked a cheap weekend flight to Dublin and a room in a modest hotel, the Grove, at the eastern end of Malahide.

I would have less than two days there, but at last I was going to visit Mary's home and see it for myself. All at once there seemed to be a kind of sense behind all those months of trying and waiting, and all the frustration and depression. It was as if this had all needed to happen in order to reinforce my motivation to take what was for me a psychologically huge step – as well as an expensive one.

Now, not only would I be able to check specific details and landmarks from my memories, but my actually being there might prompt new memories that could help in the search for Mary's family. I would also be able to take photographs, which might prove useful. I could not possibly check everything in one weekend, so I had to decide on my priorities. I wrote innumerable lists. First was the cottage in Swords Road, which held the dominant place in my memory. I even started dreaming about it – that it had been pulled down and that only the foundations remained, hidden beneath clumps of grass and buttercups. Curiously, there were always people with me during these dreams; for once I was not alone.

The second clearest picture in my mind was the church in Church Road. I hoped to compare it with my mental picture of it and the drawing I had made. My other main images were of the butcher's shop, the jetty and the railway station. Would the rest of the village seem as familiar to me? I had waited all my life to go on this trip, short though it would be. I feared failure or disappointment, but I also realised that success could bring its own problems, both for me and for the family, should they be found.

During the week before the trip the stress brought on a severe recurrence of a back problem I had had since being hit by a car in my teens. For several days I was unable to stand, and could only crawl a short distance in considerable pain. As the weekend would involve a lot of walking I feared I would have to cancel my visit. Two days before the flight I had a particularly bad night, most of it spent on the floor forcing my spine against the hard surface. But, while I lay there, something strange happened: the combination of pain and fatigue lifted me into a slightly detached and calmer frame of mind. I felt that if I was meant to go to Ireland I would be able to stand up in the morning. If I couldn't, I would have to accept that the trip was not meant to happen. In the morning I found that I could stand. It seemed like a confirmation that I was doing the right thing.

Before I left I got some medication from the doctor, and had some manipulation from a physiotherapist – not admitting to either that I was planning to fly to Ireland for the weekend. After doing some exercises, I was just able to carry a small bag and remain seated for a time. I was not comfortable, but nothing would stop me now.

It was only a ten-minute drive from Dublin Airport to the hotel – the taxi driver had no idea where it was, so I directed him from my street map. We travelled through Swords first, and then turned right towards Malahide, along the very lane in which I felt the family had lived. It was a dull, wet evening, but I was too excited for that to matter. As we went over a small bridge – across my stream? – I strained to see any old buildings that might possibly be Mary's cottage. Through the rain-streaked windows I glimpsed one likely candidate on the right-hand side of the road and in the hoped-for style and position, but we passed it too quickly for a close look.

When I reached the hotel it was twilight, and by the time I had had some coffee and sandwiches it was completely dark. There was no point in trying to do anything now, so I went stiffly to bed. But I slept very little. I was in Malahide at last!

On the Saturday morning I started out early, letting myself out by a side door, as none of the hotel staff were up. I set off eagerly, wearing a rucksack containing sandwiches, camera, notebook and map. The nearest remembered landmark was the jetty, so I turned out of Grove Road into James Terrace, where the jetty stood.

The jetty itself turned out to be quite modern, built of concrete, but it could have replaced an older, wooden one. From here the coastline curved away to the east out of the estuary towards the open sea. Struggling to remain objective, I was aware of a strong and ridiculously comforting sense of familiarity. I remembered again waiting at dusk, wrapped inadequately in a black shawl as the cold sea breeze blew inland. I still could not remember whom I was waiting for.

From the jetty I moved on towards Church Road, running north to south through the centre of Malahide, which I had mentioned under hypnosis and marked on my childhood maps. I knew there were a number of shops at its north end. Most of the buildings I came across were old, and many had obviously been shops for quite some time. But it was only under hypnosis that I had described a butcher's shop, on the west side, about second or third from the corner at the north end.

As I looked across the street I could see that there was still a butcher's in the same position. It was stone-built, and old enough to have been standing at the time I remembered. The rendering on the front was chipping away at the corners to reveal ageing stone beneath, and the windows were now large modern ones, but otherwise it looked pretty similar. I asked someone about the shop and was told that it had been there at least sixty years. Only several years later did I realise that this butcher's was quite new, though in an old building. The shop the person had been talking about – the butcher's that Mary knew – was in a similar position, but in the next road. This was one occasion when my memory of Malahide was inaccurate.

However, at that moment, the layout of the centre of

Malahide was so familiar that I was flooded with relief. As I stood there with thudding heart, thoughts came to me of Mary shopping. Quite why I remembered a butcher's shop I don't know, as there was never enough money to buy meat – any meat we had was usually rabbit or wild birds caught in the snares the children set in the fields. A memory flickered through my mind of cooking a stew containing more potatoes than meat, and I felt a frisson of fear that it would not be ready in time.

Suppressing the memory – why was it of *fear*? – I decided to go further along Church Road and see if I could recognise the church there, the first of three churches to check. As I walked I had an overwhelming sense that this was a road walked regularly by Mary; the older buildings looked very familiar.

When I reached the church itself, I stopped, spellbound. Under hypnosis I had given a fairly detailed description of the outside of the building, and later had drawn it, though with my usual lack of confidence I had anticipated only a rough similarity. But here before me was the large, plain gable end I had described to Jim, with coping stones along the top and an integral pillar at each end topped with a stone. In front was a noticeboard, not the original wooden one I remembered, but quite possibly a replacement in the same position. I felt sure that this was a building Mary had often passed rather than entered – but where would she have been going?

The sight of the church, St Andrew's, represented a wonderful confirmation of the accuracy of my memories. I found myself trembling with excitement. It proved that all the dreams, memories and images released by hypnosis were based on reality. That meant there was a real chance of my being able to trace the children. I could not wait to head for the lane where the cottage had stood. Without thinking, I turned to the left, automatically expecting to take a shortcut that I knew to be there. But, as I looked along the side of the church, I realised that the route was no longer a public thoroughfare. So I retraced my steps up Church Road, intending to check the other churches and the station on the way to Swords Road.

The first church I came to was St Sylvester's, a large, ornate Catholic church, with a garden and a sweeping drive. Since I had always thought of Mary as Catholic, I would have expected to recognise it, but I didn't, although I did remember Mary walking to church. Perhaps the Mass was more important than the building it took place in. I seemed to remember standing talking in front of a church before going inside; there was no room in front of St Andrew's for people to gather, so perhaps this memory related to St Sylvester's. I stood there, hesitant. I wanted to go in, but streams of people were entering and leaving; not only do I feel daunted by crowds, but I didn't want to interrupt any service that was taking place. The priest would be fully occupied, and in any case this church belonged to my past time and to a faith that was unlikely to accept the truth of my memories.

Knowing I was perhaps missing out on a huge opportunity, I turned and walked along The Mall towards the point where it became the Dublin Road. I passed the railway station, which was just as I had described it, set back from the road. The third church, a few yards further on, was a small, very pretty Presbyterian chapel set back from the road; it was too new to have been there in the 1920s.

Now at last I could set my sights on the cottage. I walked almost a mile to the beginning of Swords Road, where I knew it had stood. On the right I passed some new housing developments and a petrol station; the left side was bordered with ancient hedging and trees for about a hundred yards before more new houses appeared. Beyond these, the hedgerows returned and I felt much more at ease. Behind the hedge were trees, and remnants of an old stone wall, lower than I remembered, some of it falling down. There was a small, gate-sized opening with the remains of stone piers.

I was confused and uncertain. I was still hoping to find the cottage standing, and my mind could not cope with the difference between my memories and what was there now. Perhaps my recent dreams had been telling me the truth – that only the foundations remained. On the other side of the road were an old hedge and one remaining boggy meadow, through which ran the stream – so I was in the right place: the stream had been to the west of the cottage. I gazed at the trickle to which it had reduced and my thoughts turned to the children, particularly the oldest girl, who would so patiently and willingly fetch water to help Mary.

Hoping against hope, I crossed the bridge over the stream and approached the old building I had seen fleetingly from the taxi the night before. But somehow it didn't fit – neither its appearance nor its position was quite right. Just beyond it was a farm, which seemed fairly old, but when I walked into the yard I was deterred by two large dogs, which had no intention of letting anyone come close. So I took a few photographs and decided to make enquiries later by letter. Since this was the only old building left in the lane, it might still be the home of someone who had lived here in the 1920s.

I set off towards the hotel with some disappointment. A light rain started to fall, refreshing and gentle, and, as I tried to make some sense of my thoughts, I began to experience a feeling of calm, and even happiness. I stopped for a coffee in a café opposite the butcher's and started writing up some notes on the morning's findings. I had been able to walk round the village as though I knew it, the memory of how it had been strangely combined with the present. I had expected to recognise it only in part, but I *did* know the village.

Back at the hotel at lunchtime I ordered some sandwiches at the bar. They were brought by a friendly man in his early thirties, who asked if I was on holiday. I found myself opening up to him, and even explained that I had had memories of a life in Malahide since early childhood. He was fascinated, and seemed quite able to accept that my research was genuine. Afterwards I was concerned that I had been too open, but then I realised that our conversation had an advantage, for it provided a witness to my search. I asked the barman if he would have any objection to confirming the content of our conversation, should anyone want to check up on my visit; he had none.

That afternoon I wandered through Malahide, looking again at the places I recognised, hoping that new pictures or memories might emerge. It crossed my mind that I could look for a grave, but I was not sure where Mary might have been buried – and I was still not sure that the only surname I had, O'Neil, was right. I spent the rest of the weekend walking, looking, feeling, remembering – I probably did too much walking, because my backache returned, and I was glad when it was time for me to catch my plane back. When I telephoned home, Steve said, 'I suppose you've found everything and want to come home now.' I had not realised that he had so much confidence in the project.

My visit to Malahide was important. Things that had until then been just images in my mind suddenly became realities and therefore more valid. At last I felt there was enough confirmation for me to trust myself and push on in earnest.

I was standing in a portal between memory and reality; it was clear at last that the only gap between the two was of time, of past and present. A tension within me had eased, to be replaced by confidence. It was almost as though I had been told firmly, 'Of *course* it's all here! Now get on with the job and stop worrying!'

★　★　★

During the weeks that followed, my need to talk to anyone and everyone about the experience brought a surprisingly positive response. My friends were interested in hearing about it, and their encouragement and support enabled me to discuss aspects of my search that I had been hesitating to speak about, in particular the ideas and theories supporting reincarnation. It was not my place to try to change people's personal beliefs; but one day I might have to talk about all this with Mary's children, so any discussion of the subject was a useful rehearsal.

I was starting to wonder how I could introduce myself to them, or if I should do so at all. These people had suffered a major loss in childhood. Did I have the right to cause them any more unease? Would it be fair to mention reincarnation at the outset? Or should I let them draw their own conclusions without imposing my ideas? Questions that had never occurred to me before suddenly seemed very important, and the responsibility felt enormous.

However, my newfound confidence could not be punctured. I knew now that the search for Mary's children could really begin. Somewhere there were people who could answer my questions.

At this point in the search – towards the autumn of 1989 – I assumed that finding out about Mary's family would be a lengthy process. As it happened, I was wrong. I suddenly realised I was not using all available resources. I belonged to Mensa – why not contact members better geographically placed than I was who might be willing to help? I wrote letters to two members living near Malahide, and was surprised and delighted when not only did they both answer, but one gave me the name of the owner of the old building in Swords Road, a Mr Mahon.

I immediately wrote off to him asking about the building – whether it had been there for long, if it had once been used as a cottage, and whether he remembered a family who had lived in a cottage in that lane, who had five or more children whose mother had died in the 1930s. His reply came back fairly swiftly. The building had been erected by his father in the 1930s, *after* the period I was researching, and had always been used as a barn. He also gave me details of the houses in Swords Road at that point, constituting a small hamlet, which appeared on the map as Gaybrook. (This was why the name seemed so familiar to me; *inside* I had always known that this was where Mary had lived.) And, most importantly, he told me that the house I had asked about was the only one in the lane with a large number of children, whose mother had died in the 1930s.

The jigsaw pieces were beginning to fit! I hastily wrote again, communicating a few more details, including the name Mary. I asked if Mr Mahon knew anything about the husband and what had happened to the children. My main hope was that he could tell me the family's surname.

As I impatiently awaited his reply, Colin Skinner, the theology student we met in Chapter 4, contacted our friend in common, Mr Coulter. He had found the church in Malahide that I had described to him; apparently, he had recognised it immediately, which delighted me. It was a piece of independent confirmation, which I had hoped for. He had got no further with research in the church itself for, as I already knew, St Andrew's was not the one in which records of Mary's family were kept. Nor, as I was soon to find out, was O'Neil the family name. This meant that Mr Skinner had been searching for records in the wrong church under the wrong name. Nevertheless, finding the church so similar to the drawing I had sent him, which he knew I had drawn from dreams, had rekindled his enthusiasm, and he too had been writing letters of enquiry.

Not long afterwards I received a second letter from Mr Mahon. To my joy, he could remember the names of every family who had lived in Swords Road in the 1920s, and enclosed a list. A total of nineteen families had lived over an area of one mile on the road from Malahide to Swords. What was more, he gave details about the family he had mentioned before, which seemed remarkably – and terrifyingly – similar to my memories. Part of his letter read:

Relating to the mother who died in the 1930s – she was Mrs SUTTON.

I believe her husband was a British soldier in the 1914–18 war. After her death the children were sent to orphanages – later their eldest daughter MARY returned to the home. I believe the husband returned to the UK to train soldiers, 1939–45. Their children attended the Roman Catholic schools but perhaps their father was a member of the Church of Ireland.

This was truly exciting! Having the name at last was an enormous step forward, and the rest of the information explained a lot that had been puzzling. I had always felt that Mary's husband was an outsider, and had had some involvement in the First World War, in which Ireland was neutral. It would make sense for him to have been a British soldier. And the oldest daughter, as I had thought, was named Mary.

Less good news was that the children had been put into orphanages, in the plural, which meant that they had probably been separated at this traumatic time. I had had good reason to worry about their welfare. Why had their father not kept the family together? He seemed to have played little part in the children's care, and always insisted that they be quiet when he came home from work – but surely he could not have just stood by and let them be taken away, could he?

In some ways I began to feel worse. I had to accept that this was the family I had been searching for, the details were totally convincing. My whole life had been spent worrying about the children, but my concern was of no help to them. At the same time, I felt an element of relief. One of my most constant fears had been that the oldest daughter, Mary, would have been expected to take over and care for the others. At least she would have been looked after for a while, until she returned home. It seemed a preferable outcome. My sense of relief, though, seemed greater than justified by this; I fully understood it only much later, when the final pieces of the jigsaw were being slotted into place.

Meanwhile, I checked all the information I had acquired against my memories, to be certain that there really was a match. Checking and rechecking were essential as each new piece of evidence arrived; it was important to remain as objective as possible.

I wrote to thank Mr Mahon, and at this point decided to explain to him exactly what I was trying to do, and why. I did not want to mislead anyone, even if telling the truth resulted in making my job harder. I had another motive, too. This man had obviously known the family, and would be about the same age as the children. It might make it easier for the family to adjust to the idea of me and my memories if there was someone they could talk to about it.

Now that I had a surname, I decided to search the records again. At the local library the Dublin directory was missing, which meant making a lengthy expedition to the nearest main library, about fifteen miles away. However, the journey gave me time to think. I had intended to write to everyone named Sutton in the Dublin area but, as I unwound during the drive, I realised that it might be wiser to start by approaching just two or three. I listed all the Suttons, but chose only three to write to, with a letter similar to the one I had sent to the O'Neils.

I also wrote again to the first Mr O'Neil, with whom I had had no contact for nearly a year. I felt he had been interested enough to deserve a further explanation, together with my latest findings, although I did not expect him to respond. Shortly afterwards I had a letter from the Malahide local-history society. Two people had contacted them in connection with my enquiries about the old building in Swords Road – and one of them, I was delighted to discover, was Mr O'Neil. I had half expected him to shrug me off as that crazy woman again – but he had believed me, and believed *in* me. The other was one of the Mensa members I had written to.

Old Malahide Historical Society, unaware of the real nature of my enquiry, had gone to some trouble to find out about the building, but their efforts were directed at the barn, not Mary's cottage. They also told me that they were studying local records in schools and churches, and offered to pass on any relevant information. I thanked them for their help and gave further details of the family.

Throughout December, several letters passed to and fro. The three Suttons replied to say they had no connection with the family. This was disappointing, but I was struck by their helpfulness – particularly in light of the earlier lack of response to my enquiries. Perhaps my latest letters had been imbued with my recently acquired confidence in myself and my memories. One of the three, a lady from Enniskerry, Co. Wicklow, offered to look through papers in the Dublin Record Office; I told her that I had written there myself, with the new name and approximate dates, but if they were unable to help I would be happy to accept her kind offer.

Around Christmas she wrote saying that the Record Office was able to provide only a limited search, and would require precise dates. The Record Office confirmed this and told me that in any case they did not engage in genealogical research.

So, feeling a bit awkward, I enlisted the help of the lady from Enniskerry. It was unbearably frustrating not to be able to do the research in person.

Then I thought of another potential source of information: the orphanages the children had been sent to. After again trawling through the telephone directory, I started to write to all the orphanages and children's homes in the Dublin area – fourteen letters in all – asking for any information that could relate to children of Mary Sutton, who died in the early 1930s.

My research had now lasted several years, during which alternating between determined ebullience and nervous anticipation had become a repetitive cycle. Waiting for records to be uncovered was nerve-racking. I could not begin to feel at ease until there was some definite, documented proof of my family's existence.

The unusual nature of the project gave me the idea that sharing the experience with a wider audience could help to normalise it. I had kept notes the whole time, and began to feel that, if I could make coherent sense of them, they might be of interest to others in published form. This possibility gave me something else to think about; it also gave me the chance to consider how best to approach the family. I did not expect our first contact to be easy.

My greatest hope was for us to meet face to face: it is easier to look into another person and see the truth in their words, however strange, than to be contacted by letter or even telephone. I was worried not so much about explaining myself, but about the difficulties they might have with what I was saying. Any means of easing the way was worth considering.

I considered contacting a priest. Mary was Catholic, and

according to Mr Mahon the children had attended the Catholic school. I realised that I needed approval. The part of me that was Mary wanted reassurance, and my present self needed to know if it was possible to rationalise the phenomenon. While the obvious explanation, reincarnation, might not be acceptable, perhaps a broader interpretation might exist. If a priest could accept my story without condemnation, I would feel more secure.

I also considered writing a letter for the children, to be included in my account of the story. If I failed to trace them, at least they might read it if my story was published. Then I realised that the whole account (which became the book *Yesterday's Children*) would be written for them and to them. By reading it, they would know what the search had meant to me, and what *they* meant to me. They would know enough about me to decide whether they wanted contact; the option would remain theirs.

However, there was a less positive aspect to going public. While publicity might help me to find them, the family might be alienated by learning about the story indirectly before I had a chance to give them my views. Once again, burdened with endless possibilities, I was beginning to suffer from stress, with odd infections, irritability and tiredness.

During this time replies were coming in from the orphanages I had written to. Most reported no Suttons listed for the period concerned. Then, before I could become despondent again, the next piece of the puzzle arrived.

On 18 February 1990 I received a letter from a priest in charge of a boys' home in Central Dublin. The Sutton children were not listed in his records, and most of the local orphanages existing in the 1930s had closed down. His own boys' home was also closing down, so had I written a few months later I would not have had this reply. However, he had already made enquiries of the Department of Education (responsible for all admissions to state-controlled orphanages), and of the church in Malahide, and had acquired records of baptism for most of Mary's children. He enclosed copies of these, along with a note, part of which read, 'John Sutton and his wife Mary (née Hand) were not natives of Malahide, Co. Dublin, but came to live in the lodge of Gaybrook House, Swords Road. Six children were christened in St Sylvester's Catholic Church, Malahide.'

Then followed a list of six of Mary's children – *my* children:

1. John James (1923), married Sarah O'Reilly

2. Philomena (1925), married Tom Curran

3. Christopher (1926)

4. Francis (1928), married Mary Mulligan

5. Bridget (1929)

6. Elizabeth (1932), married Thomas Keogh

At last I had a real hope of tracing the family.

CHAPTER 6

Finding My Family

With this wonderful confirmation from the priest, all my doubts and fears and relentless self-questioning seemed to fade away. I felt extremely happy, as at last my goal seemed within reach. I rushed a copy to the lady in Enniskerry before she embarked on her research, and wrote to about twenty people from my list of Suttons from the Dublin directory, giving the names and birth dates of the six children and asking them to contact me if they belonged to this family. I then went back to the library and copied the addresses of all the people with the right surname and initials in the whole of the rest of Ireland. In all, I wrote to thirty-five Suttons with the same initials as the sons, and eighteen people called Keogh, Elizabeth's married name.

I decided to explain to the Dublin priest that my knowledge of this family came from dreams and memories – partly because he had asked about my connection, but principally because I felt duty-bound to do so, whatever the consequences. It was not easy but I felt in need of the support, or possibly the approval, of someone who might help me to communicate with the children. And the part of me that was Mary needed to discuss the whole thing with a priest. His reply was wonderful – positive, constructive and considerate. He had looked at the story without prejudgement and I greatly valued his acceptance of what he called 'this extraordinary phenomenon'.

On 3 March I received from the lady in Enniskerry a copy of Mary's death certificate and the birth certificates of John and Elizabeth, together with records for the six children who had been christened at St Sylvester's Catholic church in Malahide. I still felt there could be more children yet to find. The last child, Elizabeth, was born on 19 October 1932 and Mary had died on 24 October, at the age of thirty-five. The death certificate described her as Mary Sutton of Gaybrook, Malahide, a labourer's wife. She died at the Rotunda Hospital 'in the District of North City No. 2 in the Union of Dublin in the County of Dublin'. I remembered white paint and tall windows letting in lots of light.

The cause of death – which I had often wondered about – was given as gas gangrene, septic pneumonia and toxaemia. I remembered illness following a period of tiredness, which could have been caused by the toxaemia. Pneumonia would have caused the fever and shortness of breath, and gas gangrene would have caused great pain as well.

At last I had the written proof I had been seeking. Looking back over the details, I had got some names wrong but not much else. The map had been accurate; very importantly, the name Mary was right; and the letter from the priest confirmed the location of the cottage on the south side of Swords Road – though I had yet to confirm that it was the first building in the road. And the priest's letter had confirmed that the family were not native to Malahide, and that Mary's husband had fought in the First World War.

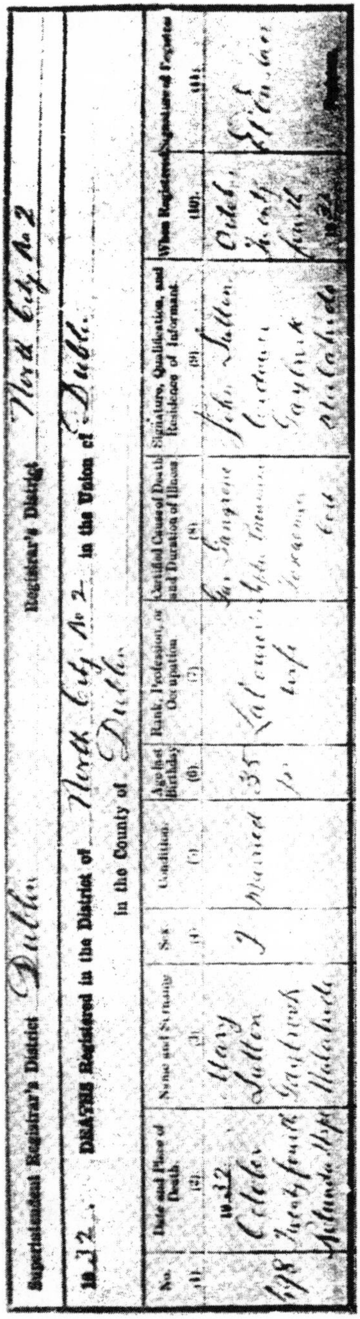

Superintendent Registrar's District Dublin — Registrar's District North City No 2

1932. DEATHS Registered in the District of North City No 2 in the Union of Dublin in the County of Dublin

No. (1)	Date and Place of Death (2)	Name and Surname (3)	Sex (4)	Condition (5)	Age last Birthday (6)	Rank, Profession, or Occupation (7)	Certified Cause of Death and Duration of Illness (8)	Signature, Qualification, and Residence of Informant (9)	When Registered (10)	Signature of Registrar (11)
198	1932 October Twenty fourth Rotunda Hosp	Mary Sutton Gaybrook Malahide	F	Married	35 yrs	Labourer's wife	[illegible] Gangrene [illegible]	John Sutton Widower Gaybrook Malahide	October twenty fourth 1932	[illegible]

Mary's death certificate

Under hypnosis I had named four of the children as James, Mary, Harry and Kathy. James was John's second name; the oldest girl – confirmed as Mary by Mr Mahon – must have been born before the family moved to Malahide. I seemed to remember the actual moving day, when Mary had one or more children in her arms.

I kept trying to picture the children in my mind in case I could pinpoint anything specific that might help them to recognise themselves in my descriptions. The youngest boy used to run his hand along the bottom of his jacket, playing with the hem. Perhaps he still did. And could he still be a bit of a loner? The confidence and straightforwardness of the oldest boy were memorable, as were the humour and resilience of the second. Talking with me while my daughter was playing with the baby doll of my childhood, my mother remembered that I had called the doll Elizabeth, the name of Mary's youngest child. Once more I wondered whether Elizabeth had had the blonde hair and blue eyes of this cherished toy.

Answers began to arrive to my letters, though with no real news; I wrote a similar letter of enquiry to the Dublin *Evening Press*, which was published early in 1990. I also wrote to Dr Ian Stevenson, the leading authority on past lives at the University of Virginia, and to Dr Peter Fenwick, a psychologist at the London Institute of Psychiatry, who had been named in a recent BBC documentary about reincarnation.

I hoped that Dr Fenwick might be able to put me in touch with someone who could help both me and the family through what might be a difficult encounter. I was beginning to panic, still questioning whether I had any right to disturb Mary's children or, conversely, whether I had the right to keep the story from them. At the root of my anxieties was still the feeling of maternal protection, even after all this time: I must not distress the children.

Both Dr Stevenson and Dr Fenwick expressed interest in my story, and the latter advised me to write to Gitti Coats, a researcher working on a projected BBC TV documentary series covering the paranormal. They could not guarantee that my case would be included in the series, but Gitti and I exchanged detailed letters and had several telephone conversations. She seemed very understanding, but I still feared inconsiderate public exposure. Once again, I began to feel tired and stressed.

Despite all my careful preparation, my first contact with Mary's children came by accident. On 20 April, obviously in response to the letter in the newspaper, I received an anonymous note postmarked Dublin. It contained a scrap of envelope on which was written the name and address of Tom Sutton; this was not a name on the list I'd been given, but I wrote to him anyway. Shortly afterwards, as I returned home from work, Steve told me he had taken a call from a telephone box in Ireland; the caller had told him that she belonged to the family I was seeking, and had rung up out of curiosity.

When she rang back, I found myself speaking to the daughter of one of Mary's sons. She told me that Mary had had eight children – so I had been right! Her father was John, Mary's second son, who spoke to me briefly himself. Quite reasonably, they were most interested in my connection with the family, but I was finding the situation much harder than I had expected. Stricken with nerves, I did not explain myself very well. I said, 'I know it's going to sound very strange, but I remember the family through dreams.'

The daughter's response was a cautious but gentle, 'Oh, yes?'

To reassure her, I described several of the children and mentioned that as a child her father had been rather mischievous, with a terrific sense of humour. With some surprise, she told me that he was still the same, and confirmed my descriptions of some of the other brothers, including the youngest being a loner. Despite her puzzlement, she gave me various family details and the addresses and telephone numbers of two of the brothers, Sonny and Francis (Frank). All four sons – Sonny, John, Christopher and Frank – had met up a few years before, but contact with the girls had been lost after they were sent to a convent school.

I promised to explain more as soon as possible, and later sent a copy of the diary I had kept covering the progress of the last few years. I preceded it with a short letter trying to explain my motives – though I was quite sure Mary's children would think me some kind of lunatic.

Nevertheless, with this contact, something had changed. I was at last able to accept emotionally that Mary's family had grown up. My feelings remained strongly maternal, but I was able to take on board that the 'children' were now self-sufficient, and I felt curiously free. I was aware, though, that I had imposed myself on the family in order to gain my own freedom from the past. I still felt a mother's sense of responsibility for them.

I heard nothing more from John or his family, which did not surprise me. But, after looking at the addresses they had given me, I decided to get in touch with Sonny, Mary's eldest son, since he lived in England and was within reach if he was willing to see me. On Tuesday, 15 May 1990, I gathered my courage and dialled his number.

When Sonny answered I heard a soft voice with a strong trace of a southern Irish accent. Remembering how direct and straightforward he was as a child, I knew that I would have to be succinct. It wasn't easy. But once more I explained that I remembered the family through dreams, telling him very briefly about my memory of the cottage, and that I believed it was first on the left.

This conversation was much easier than I had dared to hope: seventy-one-year-old Sonny took my strange call in his stride, and seemed to have no problem with what must have been a bizarre concept, right out of the blue. Straightaway, he told me I was right about the position of the cottage. I was thrilled – this was the first time I had had this confirmed. Then, briefly, he told me where the family members were or were thought to be.

Contact between the brothers had been re-established only in 1985, when Christy, the fifth child, had set out to trace the others after returning to Ireland from Australia, where he had been working as a heavy-machine operator. (Coincidentally – or synchronistically – this was around the time that I was embarking on hypnosis with the aim of tracing the family.) The eldest daughter, Mary, had died at the age of twenty-four – before I was born. On learning this, I had to push aside my grief, to cope with it later.

We did not speak for long, but Sonny said he would like to see me and talk further. Excited and indescribably happy, I said I would arrange a meeting as soon as possible. I had been keeping in close touch with Gitti Coats, the TV researcher, in case the story was to be included in the documentary, and next day I contacted her with this new development. After consulting her producer, she suggested that they interview Sonny before I met him. Sonny agreed, so once more I had to wait, something I have always found hard. I was asked not to make further contact until she had asked Sonny some questions and compared his answers with the information I had already given.

Sonny seemed happy to appear on camera, so they had to organise a film crew to be there at our first meeting. This would take a few weeks, during which there was still to be no contact between us so that the details could be analysed properly without our being able to make comparisons. It actually took four long months, during which Gitti and I exchanged numerous letters and phone calls, and she also kept in touch with Sonny. There were times when I grew fractious through frustration.

Finally, after numerous delays, some provisional dates were given for filming. A few days later Gitti rang and with many apologies told me that we would not now be included in the programme. This was partly due to politics, partly because the cottage was no longer standing – and television needs visual input. Disappointed though I was, this meant that at last Sonny and I were free to meet. I telephoned Sonny to ask if I could visit him and it was arranged for the next weekend. For the rest of that week, I willed time to pass. I could not wait to meet the boy, the man, whom I had known in my dreams for so long.

On 23 September 1990, my family and I made the three-hour journey to Leeds, to meet Mary's son. I was visibly shaking as we arrived at his house in the city outskirts. Sonny answered the door with a warm smile, and his gentle manner instantly put me at my ease. He was slightly less than average height and his slim build suggested a life of physical activity. While his wife handed round tea and talked with Steve and the children, I told Sonny more about my dreams and the memories that had led me to search for him and his siblings.

Despite my obvious nervousness, Sonny was quite relaxed. He asked me how I could explain my memories; carefully, I said that for me, it had to be reincarnation, but that other people might see it differently. He thought about this and, to my enormous relief, seemed happy to leave it at that. It was a curious situation: Sonny was old enough to be my father, yet as he told me about his life I felt what can only be described as maternal pride at all he had achieved – and anguish when he later talked about his worst times. As we talked, my daughter cuddled up to me, her closeness comforting.

Gitti had sent us a long list of the details she had compiled from both of us, which we could now compare, point by point. We used it as a starting point for our talk, but for me the joy was in simply being there. I had already read through the list in detail; Sonny's reaction to each piece of information was one of wonder, and enthusiasm.

First we talked about the cottage. It had been the lodge to Gaybrook House, and Gitti had found out that both were demolished in 1959. I had described it as single-storey, brown or buff in colour, but perhaps white. Sonny told me it had occasionally been whitewashed and was not thatched; the roof had a pronounced dip in it – as I had remembered. Also as I remembered, each of the two rooms went from front to back, with a wooden partition just inside the front door so that people had to turn left or right to go in. There were also some attached outbuildings.

Sonny's description of its location in the lane tallied with mine, and we had both described the patch of land beside it used for growing vegetables, and the stream running towards the sea, flowing under a bridge on the lane. I had said that the cottage was rented from a man nicknamed Mac; it was in fact owned by a family called MacMahon, who also owned Gaybrook House. We had both mentioned the wetlands across the road – called 'the Bottoms' by the family – and the woodlands nearby, where Sonny remembered playing as a child. He had owned the black dog that I remembered.

When I brought up Mary's waiting on the jetty, alone at dusk, Sonny became really animated. He showed me a map of Malahide, confirming that the jetty I had visited had once been wooden. 'I'll tell you why you remember that,' he said. 'As a boy I used to caddie on the island for the golfers, and at dusk my mother would wait for me on the jetty so that we could walk home together.' He used to earn 2s 6d (12.5p), two shillings (10p) of which he gave his mother. So I *had* been waiting for a boat, the small rowboat ferry, and Sonny agreed that the sea breezes would have made it cold.

We talked about the fields and woods around the lodge. The children would trap pheasants using brown-paper sugar bags containing corn, or a flashlight to dazzle them at night – this was virtually their sole source of meat. One item in Gitti's list was the description of finding the trapped hare (see Chapter 4). I described its position, adding that it was early morning and that Sonny was about eleven. Sonny just looked at me blankly and said, 'How did you know that?' The hare had still been alive, as I had said under hypnosis. This small, private incident was the first piece of information that really shocked him by its accuracy.

We talked about food: the main daily meal had consisted of potatoes boiled in their skins with butter and a jug of buttermilk. Sonny started to describe the porridge his mother made for breakfast, made of pinhead oatmeal – he did not need to complete the description; I have used pinhead oatmeal myself and know that it makes a thicker, more substantial porridge than other kinds of oats.

I was feeling quite exhilarated: so many of Sonny's facts matched my memories exactly – such as the range in the fireplace, with a hob on either side and a hook down the chimney for pots. We could easily have been reminiscing about our shared past in a normal way.

My descriptions of the children turned out to be accurate on the whole. Sonny remembered the youngest son, Francis, as quiet, and his habit of fidgeting with his clothing. The pretty little blonde girl turned out to be the seventh child, Bridget, and baby Elizabeth, with her blue eyes and blonde hair, according to Sonny, did look like the baby doll I had cherished as a child and christened Elizabeth.

Two babies had not survived: a child between Sonny and Mary had died, as well as the son I remembered just before the last child. Sonny remembered this well; both Mary and her husband had been warned that having another baby would be risking her life. Within a year, the birth of another child caused Mary's death. Sonny still blamed his father for this.

Sonny accepted my description of Mary: she was of average height, and a sturdy, happy sort of person; she wore her long dark hair in a bun. And he agreed with my description of her clothes: the blouse with three-quarter-length sleeves gathered into a narrow cuff, the dark, calf-length woollen skirt and shawl. The friend who used to spend time with her in the house was not called Molly, as I had thought, but Mary Monahan; she also went on those vaguely remembered trips to the city, by bus on a Friday night to the market.

At this point I interrupted Sonny and described the market and the street in detail. He could not remember a postbox where I placed it, and I had not remembered tramlines, but the rest was the same, with its cobbled streets and stalls. This was a relief. I had been trying to place this market in Malahide; now I understood why I could never get it to fit. It was in Moore Street in Dublin, near the Rotunda Hospital.

The memory of Mary's father had always aroused tremendous feelings of warmth and affection. I had been uncertain what he did; now I learned that he had been stationmaster at Portmanock, southeast of Malahide; he lived in the station house. My memories of watching steam trains suddenly made sense – particularly as Portmanock was a through station where few trains stopped. His job entailed keeping the station clean and tending the fields that were part of the railway property; he did not wear a uniform, but corduroy trousers tied at the ankles with string. He was from Yorkshire, and Sonny remembered his great sense of humour.

The name of their road, which I had given as Walldown Lane, was in fact Watery Lane. Mary and her husband had lived there for a time after their marriage before moving first to Kinsaley and then to Gaybrook Lodge.

Mary's two brothers were Michael and Christopher. Michael went to Kettering in Northamptonshire, while Christopher had died during the First World War at Lucknow in India, aged nineteen. It was the picture of him in uniform that I had vaguely recalled being on the wall of the cottage.

Another photograph in the cottage was of Mary herself, her hair in a bun.

Mary also had a sister, whom I had not remembered. She had four children and lived in Malahide, on The Hill, the extension of Church Road. Sonny recalled going to visit her there, which clarified another of my puzzles – to get there, Mary would have walked past both the butcher's shop and St Andrew's Church. So *that* was where she had been going!

And at last I learned more about Mary's husband, John Sutton, memories of whom had always been so elusive. He had worked as a scaffolder, a skilled job in which he took pride. He had been a soldier in the Royal Dublin Fusiliers – he was not British but from Co. Kildare. After Mary died he had stayed on in the lodge for a few years, then he married again and went to Scotland in late 1939 or early 1940.

Sonny agreed that he was very smart-looking, fit and lean, with black hair. However, he was also a drunkard, who had been violent both to the children and to Mary, hitting her and beating them with a brass-buckled belt. At the end of the week Mary had to get her housekeeping money from him before he spent it all in the pub.

This revelation explained so many things: the overriding protectiveness towards the children, the sense of quiet caution, and even fear. As Mary, I had no recollection of the violence; similarly, in my own life, I have virtually no recollection of my father's violence. As so often happens with traumatic experiences, I had blanked it out to protect my sense of self-worth. When I realised that, as Mary, I had been carrying the same sort of repressed horror, I no longer wondered at the problems that had dominated my life.

The best thing about meeting Sonny, apart from getting to

know a lovely person, was finding out at last what happened to the family after Mary's death. Baby Elizabeth had been taken away by her paternal uncle while the father was out – Sonny had handed her over and was severely scolded by his father afterwards, though it was clearly the right thing to do. Eventually she was adopted by the brother's family, and Sonny never saw her again.

The other children were taken from their father by the authorities, as he was deemed unfit to look after them. The three boys were placed in the Artane Industrial School, a Christian Brothers' orphanage in Dublin. A year later they ran away, and were resettled in an institution further away in Cork; Sonny lost contact with them for nearly fifty years. The three girls were sent to a convent school in Booterstown, Dublin, where Sonny was able to visit them occasionally. They were at least better off than they would have been at home.

Sonny, however, still at home, got the brunt of his father's increasing violence. At seventeen, he enrolled in the Free State Army, lying about his age. From there he married, went to England, and joined the RAF. His first wife died, but later he remarried, very happily.

With Sonny gone, Mary, the eldest girl, was sent home to look after her father. Given Sonny's experience of John's brutality, I could only fear for her fate there. Eventually, she found a loving husband, but tragically died in childbirth soon afterwards. Philomena and Bridget were still in the convent when Sonny joined the army, but before he left Dublin for good they were both married with children. It was good to hear that after the trauma of the family's breaking up, they had been able to live normal lives with families of their own.

As Steve drove us home, my mind was whirling. Any worries I still had were overlaid by my joy at meeting Sonny. Our meeting had gone so well – far better than I could have imagined. For years I had been worrying about how to approach my children; Sonny had made everything easy. He had simply talked, openly and naturally, and answered so many of the questions that had been plaguing me all my life.

Two lifetimes were colliding. The years of thought, preparation and research had brought me this far. Now I wanted to know more about the years I had missed while the children were growing up. And, if it was at all possible, I wanted to find the girls.

CHAPTER 7
Reunions

For a week or so after visiting Sonny I was so happy that I didn't immediately see all the implications of our meeting. My own childhood had been so unpleasant that I still found it difficult to try to remember it, but eventually my mother provided us with a better life. Sonny, at thirteen, had lost his mother and had been left with a brutal father. And I, who cared desperately about his wellbeing, had caused him to relive the worst moments of his life.

However, on a subsequent visit I found that, although recalling his childhood had been painful, the net effect was that he had got things off his chest. He accepted me open-heartedly as Mary, and even referred to her as 'you' when we were talking about her – it came out so naturally that I almost didn't notice it. We wrote to each other frequently and over the next few years I visited him whenever I could.

In one of his letters he described his life after Mary died: 'I was only thirteen years old. I had to go to school and work in the fields and look after the home from the time I got home from school. I had to have his meal ready at whatever time he came home, if not I got a beating.'

He went to work for a farmer, where he had a hard job

loading horse-drawn carts with vegetables and walking them to the markets in Dublin, finally bringing the carts back loaded with manure late in the evening. He was paid less than a pound a week – not in cash but in cigarettes for his father, bread, tea and sugar. He often went hungry, and neighbours would feed him. At home he could expect black eyes and bruises; after a year he started sleeping out in barns or ditches, but his father would come after him and there would be more beatings. Joining the army was the best thing he could have done.

Every time we met, more of my present life would crop up in connection with the memories and with my character that tied in with the past. Mary, for example, never dared stand up to her husband; I too have always found it hard to stand up for myself, particularly in childhood – although I have learned that it is possible to put one's point over without raising one's voice, without fear of reprisal. Other details fell into place, such as the flat round bread I had described, which turned out to be Irish soda bread. And my passion for Irish folk music – I wasn't surprised to learn that the only real family outings were two or three trips a year to Crossroads, on Yellow Walls, where there was dancing to a traditional group. This was surely the occasional trip in the opposite direction from Malahide centre that I had remembered.

At Sonny's suggestion I wrote to Frank and Christopher, to put them in the picture. Neither responded; however, as a result they both resumed writing to Sonny. At least my maternal instincts had served to rekindle the family feeling. Of the four brothers, only Sonny had wanted to meet me; John had never been in touch again and Christopher preferred to get information from Sonny. But, as time went by, I was more accepted by members of the family.

In October 1990, through an advertisement in the Dublin *Evening Press*, I heard from Mary's youngest child, Elizabeth. Now Betty Keogh from Rathfarnham, she was sixty and married with six children. She was not told she was adopted, or had brothers and sisters, until she was about sixteen, and she had always wanted to find her relatives. Without explaining my involvement I put her in touch with Sonny and gave her the addresses of the other three brothers. I also wrote to Frank to let him know that I had been able to trace his sister.

At the end of December, Frank's daughters wrote to me, apologising for the delay in replying. They explained that their father was dubious and did not believe in reincarnation; they were very interested, however, and wanted to know more about their grandmother and their family history. Could I fill them in? A slow but steady exchange of letters followed, and this contact was a source of great happiness.

While searching for my other family I had compiled a huge file of letters and information – travel details, maps, certificates and all the communications with Gitti Coats. It represented proof that others might check if necessary; this could be important, since in December 1991 Piatkus Books expressed an interest in publishing the account I had been writing over the years. But mainly it was my compensation for time missed while the children grew up. By March 1992 the collection of letters had grown even larger, with additions from members of the family; I also had a family tree and many photographs.

Sonny had eight children; I met his youngest daughter, a

friendly lady of my own age, on my second visit. I was unable to trace the birth of Mary, the daughter who was born in 1922 and died at twenty-four, but I was given a photocopy of a photograph her husband had kept until he died at Christmas 1991. Through the Salvation Army I was still trying to trace Bridget – Bridie – who was believed to have gone to London in the 1950s. I was also trying vainly to trace the fourth child, Philomena, last known to have lived in Dolphins Barn Road in Dublin in 1955. Sonny gave me photographs of John, taken a few years earlier. Christopher still hoped to visit Sonny – they hadn't met since the 1985 reunion – but had to postpone repeatedly because of ill health.

The youngest son, Frank, was born in 1928; his daughters showed their trust in me by sending me his birth certificate to photocopy and return. At Christmas 1991, when we had been in touch for about a year, Frank made my day by speaking to me on the telephone; he had suffered a heart attack and had a near-death experience, which opened his mind to the possibility of the continuity of the soul.

In July 1992 Sonny visited his family in Ireland, and asked me beforehand if I could arrange some newspaper coverage – after all, he was going to see Betty for the first time in sixty years! I wrote to the *Irish Independent*, which published a short account of their reunion and mentioned the part my research had played. Sonny also met up with Christopher and Frank, though not John.

I was sad not to be there myself, but the article was followed up by a story – instigated by Frank – mentioning the reasons behind my research. This aroused a lot of interest, and prompted a lovely letter to me from Betty, who had been reassured by Sonny that I was not totally strange. But the happiest outcome was the finding of Philomena, now known as Phyllis, who was in fact living in Ireland. She contacted the newspaper and was given the addresses of her siblings.

On 4 October 1992, I met Phyllis at Sonny's house, which was a great pleasure. She was only the second of the children whom I had actually met. I was still having dreams and daydreams recalling small facets of Mary's life, which included waiting outside the local school; during our conversation Phyllis told me she remembered her mother bringing tea and sandwiches to the school gate for lunch. She also spoke about the shortcut by the side of the Protestant church, and described her sister Mary going to the water pump. The highlight of our meeting was that Phyllis had the only known surviving photograph of Mary, aged probably thirty-one, with Phyllis, aged about two. She gave a copy to each member of the family and to me. This piece of physical evidence was something I had wanted and needed. I framed my copy and couldn't stop looking at it.

We also had a very constructive discussion. Phyllis had had time to adjust to my involvement and discuss it with a priest who suggested to her that, while reincarnation was not tenable, Mary could be speaking through me to reunite the family. Obviously, this was not my view, but I was happy for there to be an explanation acceptable to Phyllis and other members of the family. This acceptance made an enormous difference to me.

★   ★   ★

In February 1993, with *Yesterday's Children* nearing publication, I visited Malahide again. My publishers, Piatkus, thought it would be useful for me to return to Ireland for a day to take photographs and perhaps see some of the places I had been unable to visit on my previous trip. (My camera on that occasion had been faulty, and I had brought back only a few usable pictures.) This time I would be driven around, and it would be possible to visit both Portmarnock and Kinsaley, where I had been told we might find Mary's grave.

Sadly, a few days before the trip, Sonny phoned to tell me that John had died. Although I had never met him, he had been the first of Mary's children to contact me, and I was hit by a sense of grief.

At Dublin Airport I was met by Genny, the Irish representative for Piatkus Books, and we drove straight to Malahide. A great deal had changed even since my visit. I had a moment of absolute horror when I saw that a large area of the south side of Swords Road had been turned into a building site – then, right at the edge, I saw the piers of the original gateway, abutted by a small section of stone wall. To the right the trickle that had been the stream was confined within a concrete conduit. Standing by the wall, I realised that through a mass of brambles, I was looking at the gable end of the lodge, my cottage. Hampered by bushes, I eventually reached it by scrambling over the wall from the road and negotiating a dilapidated wall that had surrounded the outbuilding at the back.

Then I found myself inside the shell of the cottage. For a moment or two I stood there, simultaneously aware of past and present. The ruins of that tiny cottage sharpened the focus of my memory, and I could picture the internal walls, the fireplace, and other parts that had now gone. I knew that all I needed was the chance to be there, to remember that place again, and to say goodbye. My cottage had waited there, neglected and untouched, for long enough for me to find it before the bulldozers moved in.

What used to be the garden was now overgrown with scrub and bushes. A few large trees stood where the edge of the vegetable patch had been, with open fields beyond. I told Genny of the woodland that used to be there, and the meadow by the lodge. Despite the changes, I was overjoyed to be looking at this small patch of land again, not as Mary, but as my present self.

Genny and I walked around Malahide, past all the familiar landmarks – St Andrew's Church, the butcher's shop, the jetty – and went into St Sylvester's Church. Over the course of the day we looked at several graveyards; only later did I find that Mary's grave was at the church in Kinsaley, unmarked. We found the railway at Portmarnock, but the old station house where Mary had grown up had gone. We also drove around Dublin, visiting Moore Street and the Rotunda Hospital.

At the main registry of births, deaths and marriage in Lombard Street, we found a record of Mary's marriage on 22 July 1917, witnessed by her sister and her younger brother. The wedding was at the Baldoyle church, which we visited, and where I learned that Mary's date of birth was 1 December 1895.

Possibly the best part of that day was meeting three of Mary's children at the airport before I left. Meeting Frank and Betty for the first time, and Phyllis for the second, I was profoundly aware how lucky I had been since my first nervous phone call to Sonny. I had not expected anyone to listen, but Sonny had listened. His acceptance had given me permission to express some of the feelings for the family that I had held in for so long.

Publication of the book and a publicity tour were fast approaching, and during the last week in April I went to Ireland to take part in a London Weekend Television documentary with five of Mary's children, including Christy, whom I was meeting for the first time. It was also the first time the family had been together since 1932, and they were all happy to be involved with the programme. Only Bridie was still missing. Phyllis had discovered that she and her husband had travelled to Australia in the 1950s, and the documentary editor, David Alpin, now set about making enquiries through Australian radio stations.

We had just one day's filming with the family in Ireland, but it was a very happy day. We enjoyed the opportunity to spend time together, and spent a great deal of time talking, off the camera as well as on. Each member of the family explained how they understood the phenomenon of my memory of their mother's life, ranging from an acceptance of reincarnation to the belief that Mary was speaking through me. Talking so directly felt very cleansing, and for me it was one step further along the road of understanding and acceptance.

At Gaybrook the family and I stood together in the ruins remembering how it had been. Christy, who had not returned to this spot since childhood, could remember exactly where he had been standing when his mother was carried out and taken to the Rotunda Hospital. It was the last time he had seen Mary's face, and talking about it brought him close to tears. Betty and Frank, who had been very young at that time, were uncertain about details of the layout inside the cottage; nobody found it strange that I was able to point out where the fireplace or door had been, and could talk about life there just as easily as any of the older family members.

The programme reconstructed several events using actors, and I watched one such scene on the evening before the reunion. On the jetty at Malahide an actress stood with a dark shawl round her shoulders as a small rowing boat approached. A cool sea breeze caused me to shiver as the boy playing the part of Sonny jumped ashore and hugged his 'mother'. To my surprise and embarrassment, I could not hold back my tears; I realised I was still feeling very fragile and vulnerable.

Several weeks later David Alpin telephoned to say that he had heard from a radio station in Australia. They had been called by a man who turned out to be Bridie's widower; she had died nearly twenty years before. Shortly afterwards, Sonny received a very long letter from two of her daughters, including family photographs; with Sonny's encouragement I made contact with them too.

I made several more trips to Ireland to publicise the book, and was able to take my family with me on one occasion. Sonny appeared with me on a television show while my husband and children, along with Frank, Betty, Phyllis and Christy, sat in the audience. Sonny expressed his views on reincarnation and made it clear that he accepted the concept – a public affirmation that took me a little by surprise, though it was a most welcome and warm surprise.

Before we left, Sonny and Betty both wanted reassurance that I would stay in touch with them. I was surprised and touched. Preoccupied with my own insecurity, I hadn't realised that any of the family might fear losing contact with me once the furore had died down. The only possible answer was hugs all round and an affirmative 'Of course!'

In fact we were able to see each other fairly often, and kept in touch between visits. Between the first meeting with Sonny in September 1990 and Betty's death in August 2003 I had thirteen years in which I was able to catch up with the family I had lost a lifetime before. It was fairly easy to visit Sonny in Leeds, usually with my children in tow. There were letters, telephone calls and time enough to let the strangeness of it all become less strange for everyone. An added bonus was that further television programmes required us to be together for interviews, so that we had several opportunities for the whole family to meet again in Ireland.

Finding the family at last, after such a long and tortuous journey, was a huge relief, and their acceptance and warmth were a bonus I could never have envisaged. I could finally lay Mary's guilt to rest, and I felt much more at peace with myself. I had also reached a point where I could talk about my experiences and beliefs much more openly than ever before – indeed, I had to. *Yesterday's Children* aroused a lot of interest, and I was taken aback by all the publicity, something I had not given much thought to beforehand. I had had dreams of giving interviews, but had not thought of these as premonitory. Over the next few years I had to overcome my natural shyness to meet the demand for radio and television interviews for a number of countries as well as taking part in conferences. Throughout all this I still kept up my chiropody practice.

Within the first few weeks of publication the feedback in the form of letters and calls on radio shows reassured me that I had done the right thing: so many readers felt comforted or uplifted. Best of all, it was evident that I was reaching some people who, like myself, had past-life memories and were trying to make sense of them, often in the face of disbelief or opposition.

My family reacted wonderfully to the book's success and the demands it made on all of us. They had supported me throughout my long journey – of course, for them my past-life memories had always been a part of me – and had coped well with my reunion with Sonny and Mary's other children. Publication gave my children an opportunity to consider their own views on reincarnation, and they came to the conclusion that it made sense.

What had never occurred to us was that the publicity would give us the chance to travel as a family. Members of the Sutton family were able to join us on some of these trips, and Sonny joined me on about nine different tele-vision programmes. When we went to America in May 1994, Sonny and Phyllis came too. This time my husband and son also appeared with me on *The Phil Donahue Show* in New York, and both confirmed their support of my researches. Steve joked about the situation, remarking that, just as the children were beginning to grow up and he had hoped for more time together, I had gone and found a whole other family!

It was television that brought me an opportunity for further healing. In April 1994 I was taken to the Rotunda Maternity Hospital in Dublin by the ABC News *20/20* programme for publicity for my American publishers. I had been able to sketch the location of the room where Mary died, and the hospital matron located it for me – a small isolation room at a corner of the building, one floor up, with the tall windows

I had remembered. When I entered the room I immediately began to feel increasingly ill at ease. I did a short interview, but my feelings of panic became too much to bear and I excused myself and backed out of the room.

The next day we returned for further filming and after a while there I felt less uncomfortable as I gradually started letting go of the anguish of Mary's death. Even though it was weeks before I felt completely at ease again, I was grateful that the film crew had persuaded me to find that room. It enabled me at last to let go of the sense of guilt at dying, and accept that when battling against so many physical odds it was not a sin to have given up the fight to live. I finally forgave myself completely for deserting the children through what was, after all, an inescapable death. And, by resolving this source of pain, I made room for a little more peace of spirit.

I know how lucky I was to have those years of contact. The peace of mind that came about through tracing the Sutton family made me feel more complete and changed me for the better – even though ultimately I had to learn to let go of the family members, as time took them from me. Frank died in the autumn of 2000 and Sonny early in 2002, followed by Betty in 2003. It was difficult losing the children again – particularly Sonny, with whom I had a close bond, and who had brought about my reunion with the rest of the family. But this time it was different. I now knew about their lives and their families and that at least most of them managed to live long and happy lives, despite their difficult beginnings. Best of all, with the help of Sonny's open-mindedness and warmth, I had been welcomed and included.

In retrospect I am aware that one reason I threw myself

into further research in 2002 – into my Japanese life – was to help me cope with this unavoidable loss. Loss is an inevitable part of the cycle of life, and grief is a quite natural part of the process; I think it helps us to gain perspective. I am thankful that I was able to get a second chance to see my family again and hope that one day we may cross paths again, in another life.

CHAPTER 8

A Life in Japan

Since my teens I had known that there would be two key phases in my life. The first coincided with the complex and difficult period that culminated in resolving my life as Mary, at the age of thirty-seven. The second would be between about the ages of forty-nine and fifty-four. I wondered for many years what might take place during this period, and used to discuss it with friends. I was anticipating a single event that might lead to a significant personal change, and hoped that this would not be quite as traumatic as the earlier phase. As I approached my forty-ninth birthday in 2002, I began to hope that it would mean the resolution of my memories of my life in Japan, the last bit of unfinished business from past lives that there was any chance of resolving.

Just as I had had a burning need to trace my family in Ireland, I had always fervently hoped to be able to follow up my short life in Japan. This need is difficult to explain; it is like trying to find something that has been lost – but something that is a part of you, without which you cannot feel whole. And, as my life in Ireland slipped away, my need to find a completion of my Japanese life came to the fore.

As with my memories of Mary Sutton, my memories of Japan had been with me from early childhood. They would come piecemeal – as present-life memories do – but slowly I built up the story of a Japanese girl whose name I never knew. As with my memories of Ireland, I started as a child drawing maps and pictures of the location, and many of my activities had echoes of Japanese customs.

I grew up with a passion for anything Japanese, from chrysanthemums to bonsai, often unaware of the association. When as a teenager I made bamboo flutes, I did not know until I was told that they were a traditional Japanese instrument. I sold several to Morris dancer friends who needed simple instruments, and they worked well enough. One particularly proficient flautist asked me where I had found the formula for the correct spacing of the holes. I told him I just put the holes where they seemed to need to go, an answer he found rather perplexing.

When I was about eight my father gave me a folded paper bird; I immediately unfolded it, step by step, to find out how it was made. I made dozens of origami birds in coloured paper to put all round my room, and learned how to make other things by folding paper. Then a neighbour, a keen gardener, introduced me to the delights of growing miniature trees in pots, which became a lifelong hobby. I was not deliberately seeking out Japanese interests, but found these activities reassuring.

The life I remembered in Japan ended over a hundred and twenty years ago, in the late 1800s. As it was the life immediately before Mary Sutton's, I was fairly certain of the time slot. It had to end before 1895, when Mary was born, and I have always felt that the whole life happened between about 1860 and 1880. I can't explain how I know the dates of my past lives, but my knowledge seems to be pretty accurate.

As it happens, this time span coincided with a period in Japan when the old order, the samurai caste system, was replaced with the return of imperial rule. Japan had been closed off in 1635, with no citizen allowed out of or back into the country, and was not open to foreign trade until 1859. So the late nineteenth century was a time of great change and development politically, educationally and technologically. This era, beginning in 1868 when the sixteen-year-old emperor moved to the eastern capital Edo (renamed Tokyo) is referred to as the Meiji Restoration – Meiji meaning 'enlightenment'.

My strongest memory of Japan was the view from the veranda at the back of my father's house. I was a girl living in a hillside home overlooking a small bay. The house was set above and slightly apart from a nearby village, standing at the northern end of the bay facing roughly west. I used to watch the sun setting over the water from the veranda, sinking behind a group of rocky outcrops at the far left end of the bay. I felt that there was also an island in that direction, which was either small or far away. On the right side of the bay there was a distinctive peninsula on which the house stood, near its base. The bleak rock falling away from the house looked jagged and very dark in colour; when it was wet it was virtually black. There was no beach bordering the peninsula, but there was a small beach to the left beyond the house. I also recalled hills or mountains that filled one margin of the horizon and formed a backdrop to the view.

Sketch of veranda at rear of house

The house was probably single-storey and stood alone, with perhaps four other houses nearby, which could not be seen from the veranda. The main village was in the valley slightly to the southeast, with access to the bay via a valley between the hills. There were no roads, but a track ran past the front of the house and then northwards up the coast before turning inland. From my viewpoint on the veranda I could see the land dip to my left. Where it opened out at the coast I could see fishing boats setting out or pulled up on the shore, near the small dwellings of the working people.

It is possible that the view from the veranda has always been strong in my mind because I seemed to spend a great deal of time out there just looking out at the sea. This was a special pleasure during the rainy season, as I sheltered under the veranda roof while the rain fell heavily and the mild

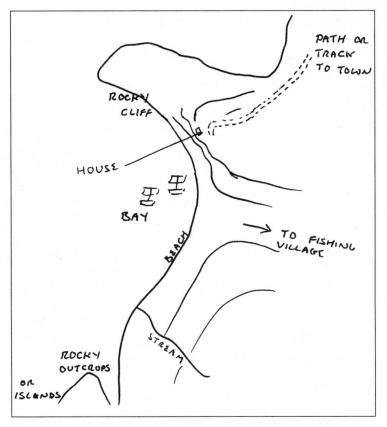

Sketch of the bay area and track passing the house

breeze from the sea made the air fresh and exhilarating. I still feel uplifted by summer rain. The veranda had a rail at the front, and the floor was uneven, made up of poles. I also recalled another slightly different floor surface probably made of poles covered by straw matting.

Our family was well-to-do, and our life seemed calm and ordered. My father had a position of minor importance, and

I was not allowed to mix with the village children, but I had several sisters and at least one brother, who was about seven years younger than I was. I have a number of isolated memories – for instance, I see in my mind a silky fabric in a soft cream colour with a design of highly coloured, long-necked birds, which may have been my mother's. Sewing was a part of my life – as it is today. The fabrics I am drawn to now often turn out to be of Japanese origin, such as highly decorative crêpe de Chine with fine-line detail.

As well as the view of the coast, my strongest memory is of a journey with my father to meet the man he had chosen to be my husband. I am fairly certain that I was seventeen at the time. We set off early one morning while the dew was still on the grass. We started along the track that passed near the house and back past the village; at first it ran close to the coast, and then meandered inland.

My prevailing memory is of riding a donkey or pony led by my father, who was looking at the ground as we walked – the track was quite rough in places. The journey to the town took about half a day; at our slow place, I have always assumed that we travelled about ten miles or so during the course of the morning. I was not being pampered by riding while my father walked: it was what I had to do – perhaps because I was dressed up and had to arrive looking my best.

I remember my father during that day. He was fairly quiet and we spoke little. I had a great deal of respect for him, but although our interaction seemed reserved I recall him with warmth and affection. I knew there was a caring side to his nature, which he preferred to keep hidden. He had a kind face, furrowed with worry lines. He seemed to have a lot of responsibilities, but would always appear calm and very controlled.

We reached a town where we left my mount behind and took a small ferryboat across a strip of sea. I had the impression that we were travelling from one island to another. We may have had to wait a while for the ferry, and I think there was some negotiation over the fee, but the crossing itself was quite short. It was afternoon when we reached the busy town on the other side, where we immediately found ourselves in a built-up area. I felt uncomfortable at the prospect of living in the town; it was all so busy, and I much preferred the country.

We walked through the narrow streets to a large house, where I was introduced to my husband-to-be. I met him only briefly, answering one or two polite questions with my head bowed. Then I was led to another room, where I sat with an elderly woman, seemingly a relative of my fiancé, while my father stayed and talked with him; presumably, they were finalising the marriage negotiations. Nervous and tense, I sat and waited for quite a while, sitting very still with my back very straight, hardly moving at all, and hardly speaking.

I was rather surprised that the man I was to marry was middle-aged – not as old as my father, but much older than I had expected. I was sure that my father would have made a good choice with my future security in mind, and this man had an excellent position. But I was feeling really unhappy about it. During our brief meeting he seemed pleasant enough, but he was not at all attractive. I was worrying, too, about leaving home and living across the water – I wondered if I would ever see my family. But I would not have dreamed of letting my father – or anyone else – know how I felt; that would have been ungrateful – indeed, unforgivable.

That night we stayed in a small lodging house nearby, in a street with a number of houses that seemed crowded together. I felt that either we could not afford to stay anywhere more grand, or this was the normal overnight accommodation for travellers. Next morning, we travelled home. There was nothing to say about the arrangement, so I said nothing about it.

Everything had been agreed, and, as a dutiful Japanese daughter, I knew the decision was not mine. But I felt frustrated and depressed. To disobey my father would be to dishonour him. I had no right to refuse the marriage, but, deep down, that was what I would have liked to do. Ashamed that such a rebellious thought could even cross my mind, I concealed my feelings out of respect for my father.

Soon I was on the ferry boat again, this time destined for my wedding. I had to go, in obedience to my father – an obedience soon to be transferred to my new husband. But my wedding was never to take place. We were close to our destination when the boat collided with a small fishing vessel whose crew were too busy arguing with each other to notice they were heading for a collision.

There was a fairly substantial thud. The ferry was crowded, some of the passengers were standing, and on impact several of us were thrown into the water – I was briefly aware of people splashing and shouting. Because I had not been allowed to play with the village children I had never learned to swim, but I should have been close enough to the boat to be pulled out of the water. Somehow, that didn't happen.

I remember a brief moment of absolute panic, which left me as my body fell limply down through the water. Then I felt very calm. The transition from unconscious body to discarnate spirit went almost unregistered; I seemed to move quite naturally into a state in which there was no fear. A light seemed to cut through the water, and I was drawn towards what appeared to be a vortex swirling anticlockwise in the water above me. I recognised this as death and freedom, and I offered no resistance as I was drawn into the vortex and peace. My recollection after that is vague, though I have a slight memory of meeting someone I knew, and then of being somewhere very bright and white with touches of blue, and totally peaceful.

I had always had very mixed feelings about this death. I often wondered whether I did not try hard enough to save myself from drowning. Since it saved me from being married to a man I did not want to be with, perhaps it was just too convenient, and even partly intentional. It may, equally, have been completely accidental. If after entering the sea I had taken a sharp breath and inhaled water, as is common in such circumstances, I would not have surfaced anyway. But I always felt some guilt about it. Whether justified or not, feelings of guilt are definitely an aid to remembering past lives, and may be my key link to that memory, as was the case with Mary.

As a child I had tried to find the location of my Japanese home by an instinctive form of dowsing, running my hand over a map and waiting to be drawn to a sensation of warmth. With my school atlas the nearest I could get was the northwest corner of Kyūshū, the southernmost island of Japan. Many years later, I was able to find slightly more detailed maps, and on these the nearest town that I could find marked was Kitakyūshū, a large city and port slightly to the east of the area of coastline I felt drawn to.

For years I looked through other people's atlases and maps in the hope of finding the bay where I had lived, but I was never able to see what I was looking for. I would bother people who had been to Japan in case they had a better map, but always without success. On some maps there was another town, named Kokura, which seemed vaguely familiar, whereas Kitakyūshū did not. Much more recently I found out that Kitakyūshū is the modern name for a conglomerate of five towns, including Kokura. I thought this might be the town where we caught the ferry on the journey to meet my fiancé. Meanwhile, my quest was only hypothetical; the reality was that Japan was a long way away and I could not see any possibility of researching that life. Then, with the success of *Yesterday's Children*, everything changed, as new opportunities opened up for me.

When I underwent hypnosis in the late 1980s, Jim never once looked at the timeframe in which the Japanese memory could have been found. It was a curious omission, but it means that the story outlined above remains as close as possible to my original childhood memories, with no additional details.

There was one moment when I might have been regressed to that life, but instead went down a completely different route. In 1996 I took part in a television programme with Dr Brian Weiss, an American psychologist and expert in hypnotic regression; some of his work involves using hypnosis to explore the root causes of phobias and fears. I had met him before, and admired his responsible approach:

as he says, anyone can use hypnosis for regression, but it is important to accompany it with good therapy, which takes aptitude and a proper training. On this occasion he was in Britain publicising his book *Only Love is Real*, describing a regression case that linked two of his patients in previous lives.

It was a long, exhausting day. I was up very early to be collected at 5 a.m. so that Brian and I could share an interview on *The Big Breakfast*, and the day ended with a radio programme at midnight, via telephone link from my home.

During the day we shared several interviews; one programme we recorded together was in the loft of a hot converted warehouse in the East End of London. It was late afternoon, and we were both tired. Although the piece was to be quite brief, the somewhat shirty young director became very demanding, endlessly repeating shots, asking inappropriate questions, and becoming quite short with us. This seemed unnecessary: Brian is the most gentle person one could hope to meet, and I am always concerned to do the right thing. In retrospect I think the subject matter made her uncomfortable.

In the end, it took about six hours to produce the final item, which lasted less than five minutes. Brian had been asked to recreate a hypnosis session with me, and we had both explained that we would not undertake actual hypnosis without the chance of a follow-up – something anyone should consider before undergoing hypnosis. However, I had not taken into account that I have never actually been able to re-enact a hypnosis session without going under, and my state of fatigue made it impossible not to succumb. I should add that my curiosity had also been aroused.

Discussing methods beforehand, I asked Brian not to relax me by using a deep-breathing method, since, if I over-concentrate on breathing, I am liable to hyperventilate. I asked him if this might be because I remembered drowning in Japan, but he told me that hyperventilation was usually associated with death by smoke inhalation in a fire. The moment he said the word *fire* I saw a brief picture of myself as a small boy in a smoke-filled room, and felt scared and claustrophobic.

When we tried the re-creation, perhaps because of fatigue, I unintentionally slipped straight into a hypnotic trance, and found myself as the small boy I had just glimpsed. I was in late-sixteenth-century France, a four-year-old in dark velvet knee breeches, hiding by a musty-smelling wooden staircase. I had glimpses of heavily curtained doors, and of my mother in an elaborate full-length gown of beaded velvet and lace, wearing a tall powdered wig. Taken to the last moments of this wealthy life, at the age of ten, I was aware of fire and smoke and of running around trying to find a way out.

Ironically, this life as the son of a French aristocrat immedi-ately followed the third past life I recalled in childhood, that of the French peasant girl who had died in poverty some nineteen years earlier. Reading my daughter's history books at the time, I found that during the French Revolution in 1789, when the homes of aristocrats were burned down, the occupants were often allowed to escape. When people died in these fires it was usually by accident.

It seems likely that a whole set of my present-day phobias may have stemmed from this frightening death – such as being trapped in small spaces, or any form of physical restriction. Of course, in this studio session we had not set out with the idea of treating my own phobias, which remained with me; strangely, perhaps, I have never considered using hypnosis for therapy.

Soon after *Yesterday's Children* came out I was twice approached by Japanese television companies with requests for an interview – the second would have involved visiting Japan. Twice I got my hopes up; twice they were dashed when the programmes failed to materialise. By the end of 1996 such requests were increasingly irregular and I did not expect any more. I tried to push from my mind the insistent urge to know more and to resolve the guilt that still haunted the memory of my death. What I really needed was luck – and eventually luck came.

Nine years down the line, a third Japanese production company asked me for an interview. I was very excited at the prospect of doing an interview for Japan – a place that had once been my home. Although I had outlined my Japanese memories in *Past Lives, Future Lives*, their agent in the USA had not come across it. When I mentioned it to her she wanted to know more, and I happily faxed her some of the details. She was interested enough to offer to look for a map of Kitakyūshū when she next visited Japan.

On 1 April 2002, a Japanese television crew came to my home and I at last recorded an interview to be broadcast in Japan. I was by now used to having TV crews in our house: I had recorded quite a number of interviews, at least half of them for foreign companies. This one was to be part of a programme about reincarnation, which would include interviews with Dr Brian Weiss, who had suggested my participation in the documentary. Obviously, I was expected to talk about my memories of Ireland, but I was also asked about my memory of my life in Japan. I did not know if they would use the footage, but I took the opportunity while on camera to describe the view from the veranda, the bay and the peninsula, and the story of my sudden death.

I was well aware that the chances of its being followed up were slim, but I was thrilled to have the opportunity of describing the place, in the slight hope that a Japanese viewer might recognise it. The following day I drew a detailed map, referring to my old notes, showing the area of Kyūshū that I felt was relevant, and a sketch of the bay (how I wished I had had it at my interview!). I sent it to Tomoe, the agent who had expressed interest in the story.

The possibility of resolving that life by tracing the location was at last beckoning. In this case, I had no wish to use hypnosis: I felt there was enough detail without trying to prise out a bit more. And experience had taught me that it can take a long time to get over the trauma of reliving the past. There always has to be a period of adjustment after concentrating on these memories, while one comes to terms with the emotional content. It is difficult enough to cope with the barrage of psychological baggage that comes when exploring a past life and unfolding memories, and I had no desire to add to this burden by opening myself up to more hypnosis.

The downside of never having used hypnosis to explore this life was that over time I might have forgotten some details, while the absence of a name could be problematic. But, as I gave more thought to it, other tiny details began to emerge from my subconscious – like memories of and feelings for family members in that life, and glimpses of their facial expressions. At the same time, thinking about it also triggered a strong emotional response, so that once again I was beginning to become obsessed. Now I did not just want to go to Japan: somehow, I *had* to go.

CHAPTER 9
Preparing to Go

To find out more about my life in Japan I was going to need luck, help and patience. I am quite good at patience up to a point, but over the years I had not even got as far as confirming the exact area concerned. One of my major stumbling blocks was the problem of finding a map with enough detail. I was quite convinced that all I needed was a map showing the peninsula, and I was pinning my hopes on Tomoe. Even so, I was not sure if a city map of Kitakyūshū would cover a large enough area to include the stretch of coastline I needed to look at. The place I recalled was very rural, and might be a long way outside the city.

On 20 April, I received a map that helped me a little. I had given a copy of my sketch map of the bay to Neil, a cycling friend of Steve's, who offered to search on the Internet for information about the city of Kitakyūshū and the area around it. I had no Internet access myself, so this was very helpful. Neil found a map showing the main features of the city, though with little detail, along with some historical notes about Kitakyūshū.

When I looked at the printout I didn't expect to see anything useful, and was surprised to see for the first time what looked very like the distinctive peninsula and bay I had been drawing and describing for some years.

As I looked at the map, I had a powerful feeling that I had done all this before – received the map from Neil, stood looking at it on the kitchen table, and seen what I had expected to find. At the same time, I felt a curious uneasiness that I can only describe as a mixture of elation and dread. It almost felt like a warning of things to come – but, if it was, it was one that I would ignore. The sense of *déjà vu* gave me the impression that it was all meant to happen.

All the details I had been able to glean so far seemed to match the topography of this very simple map. The peninsula lay to the northwest of Kitakyūshū city, and it could well be a day's walk to the narrow strip of sea dividing Kyūshū island from the Japanese mainland. But, even if I had found the right area, how could I confirm the existence of the house and discover who had lived there? I was going to need help. Suddenly, it seemed a ridiculous position to be in. All my life I had known that I had once lived in Japan, but I had never attempted to learn the language. I was totally reliant on someone showing enough interest to undertake some of the research for me.

Clearly, I had to keep trying for a proper map. I wrote to Tomoe with details, enclosing a copy of the downloaded map, and explaining,

It was the shape of the peninsula that seemed familiar, also it would put an island between the bay and the setting sun which would be right, and although it is close to Kitakyūshū the journey to the ferry would still seem far on foot. A more detailed map might be clearer but I have a good feeling about this site.

One small piece of insurance I thought worth taking out at this stage was to send as much detail of my past-life memory as I could to my publisher, with a covering letter dated 22 April 2002, before I could get any of the much-needed verification. This would provide me with a witness who would confirm seeing the written details before I could find the bay itself.

I realised that my chances of doing so were slim. As far as I was aware there was not a single case in the world of someone's having two consecutive past lives researched and verified. Yet I felt confident that something would happen. It has always been my view that if something is meant to happen it will; if not, then it won't. It took Neil to point out that this fatalistic attitude was very Japanese, in keeping with the philosophies of Shinto and Buddhism.

I tend to think that some of the events that we attribute to fate may be the result of an interaction between the conscious and the unconscious. Some happenings of course come about through our conscious decisions. But we also have a deep, hidden connection with each other and we may, without realising it, react to events occurring beyond our immediate environment, of which we have no conscious awareness. In other words, fate and coincidence may be the result of people interacting through a psychic connection that links everyone to everyone else. This would mean that, albeit unconsciously, we control our own fate and all the apparently chance things that happen to us.

This ties in with today's popular belief that we create our own destiny. In other words, if you don't decide what you want out of life you will be given only random opportunities; if you decide what you want you can achieve it by asking for it, clearly, and with positive intent. This is followed up by taking some action and you then wait for the outcome, while staying open to possibilities. A curious feature of this process is that the action itself can be general rather than specific, as though just nudging the collective unconscious will be enough to get the ball rolling.

Well, I was clear about my aim. Of course, I wanted to be able to confirm the existence of the girl I remembered being, but I realised that this simply might not be possible. More importantly, however, I wanted to achieve closure – and I was prepared, somehow, to go to Japan to do it.

One of my characteristics – possibly a failing – is that I want to do everything I can for myself. (Our house insurer once tried to sell us accidental cover by asking what I would do if I accidentally put my foot through the ceiling of the loft. I said that I would need galvanised flat-headed nails, plasterboard, jointing tapes and Artex; then I would fix it.) Given a problem, I take time to plan, and then, when I am sure about what I want to achieve and the best way to achieve it, I go all out to get it done. This is an excellent way to design and build a bookcase or a table, but it may not be the best way to do research. Yet that seemed to be the direction in which I was being impelled.

I knew what my aim was, and I had started to throw a few stones into a few ponds, so now my strategy was to take whatever action I could, followed by lots of waiting and seeing. I had experienced a number of helpful 'chance' coincidences while researching Mary Sutton's life. I had yet to see if my search for the life in Japan would be helped in the same way.

During May I knew that, before I explored other avenues, it would be prudent to wait and see if there was a response to the Japanese television broadcast; realistically, this could take several months. Meanwhile, I ordered a larger map from a new local bookshop, and the owner rang me to say he had located one in which the south island of Kyūshū would appear about nine inches long.

That evening I turned on the television and found myself watching a documentary about the transportation of one of Japan's bullet trains to the Transport Museum in York. The train travelled through Japan to the southern town of Fukuoka, which is near Kitakyūshū, a little way down the coast from what I thought of as 'my' bay. There were tantalising glimpses of the route, including one shot that I felt sure was of the railway bridge that now crosses to Kitakyūshū. Despite modern developments, the sight of the area triggered a reaction in me – a sense of familiarity. The bullet train was loaded onto a ship in Fukuoka Harbour and, as it left to travel northwards up the coast, I spotted the hummock of an island whose shape was very reminiscent of the island I used to see from the veranda. Alas, it was only a quick view.

It was as though I were being teased. Before seeing this, it had been relatively easy to be patient. Now I was itching to go – but how? My mind went round and round. Travelling to Japan would be very expensive. Steve and I are both self-employed and earn enough to pay the bills, but not to take trips to the Far East. Even if I could afford it, I would need the assistance of someone who could speak and read Japanese. And it could still all end as a complete waste of time and money – after all, the house I remembered was very unlikely to have survived. In any case, I still needed to locate the exact spot, and a detailed map was essential. No map, no trip.

For the time being I felt I had reached an impasse. My only hope was the possibility that someone in Japan might be able to provide some help, and I started asking former contacts and current friends and patients for any information they might have about Japan. I realised that every possible opportunity should be followed up. I began carrying with me copies of the list of details and the maps, along with a covering letter that could be passed on to anyone who might remotely be able to help. From this point on I was amazed at the number of people with friends or relatives who worked at least some of the time in Japan. However, most of them turned out to be in Tokyo, which is a very long way from Kitakyūshū.

By the end of June I was becoming more and more obsessed and distracted. I knew that I would be going to Japan, but had no idea how, and I was still agitating over finding a map. There had been no reaction to the Japanese documentary, and no map from Tomoe.

At the library I found some travel books on Japan, which provided some helpful information, in particular confirming some of the domestic details that I remembered. For instance, one reason why visitors remove their shoes when visiting a Japanese home is that shoes could damage the traditional *tatami*, the thickly woven rush mats that are still popular even in modern homes. One of my memories of my home in nineteenth-century Japan is the floor covering that felt like poles (which may have provided the underlying structure) and reeds; I remember the sensation of walking on what felt like reeds under my bare feet.

I also remember that the home seemed very empty of furniture. This is still the case in older, more traditional homes, where the bedding and futon mattresses are stored in large cupboards during the day, leaving the bedroom empty. In the living rooms the only furniture will be a low table surrounded by cushions to sit on. The rooms are divided with sliding *fusuma*, paper stretched on wooden frames, which gives a sense of space when everything is tided away and the partitions drawn back for the day.

I recognised this need for tidiness, for few possessions, and keeping things out of the way to maximise floor space. As someone who often clears out cupboards and constantly reorganises everything in the house, I can see that Japanese minimalism is a strong influence in my life – though not easy to put into practice in modern Western life, especially with a family.

Another small facet of social history came up on a TV travel programme, which showed a young woman trying on a kimono. The fit around the legs is close, which would make it impossible to walk long distances at any speed. This could be why I remembered travelling by donkey or pony: in full traditional dress there was no way I could have walked ten miles to the ferry. I would also have had to sit side-saddle, which would explain why I was aware of seeing my father walking on my right rather than looking straight ahead.

There was little information in the travel books about Kitakyūshū, which is now a highly industrial area, though the island of Kyūshū, with its mild climate and stunning scenery, is of more interest to travel writers. Apart from a little Japanese history concerning the Meiji Restoration, one thing I learned was that there was a revolt in Kyūshū a hundred years ago, when all the place names were changed.

As I have poor recall of the place names anyway, I thought this might not be a problem.

At my daughter's suggestion I contacted the editors of the *Fortean Times* (a British monthly magazine that deals with anomalous phenomena) in case they knew of a researcher working in Japan. I had been a reader of the magazine since giving them an interview in 1993, and had given a talk at the magazine's 1998 conference. However, this took me no further forward.

In July I celebrated my forty-ninth birthday. Having reached what I had anticipated to be a pivotal year, I found myself becoming increasingly agitated, unable to change direction but equally unable to move forward. When the map from the bookshop arrived, it still showed too little detail. It was one more cause of frustration.

During this waiting time there was yet another request for a television interview, this time for a programme for *Horizon* to be made on 30 August and aired in October. Such requests had become infrequent lately; perhaps this renewal of interest could mark the beginning of a change. The opportunity to broadcast might give me a chance to talk about Japan.

Meanwhile, I still had not given up on the possibility of going to Japan myself. I began reviewing some of the potential problems and thinking up practical measures to overcome them. The most useful thing I could have done was to try to learn some Japanese, but, having absolutely no gift for languages, I avoided thinking about it. Instead, I focused on other problems.

I have a number of allergies varying in severity. In particular I have adverse reactions to drugs, which means that I cannot visit countries where an inoculation is required, and

I have to avoid infections, because I cannot take any anti-biotics. And there is one drug reaction that is hard to avoid because the dangerous agent is often used in cooking and people are often unaware how little can set off a reaction. My allergy to alcohol is quite frightening: my pulse rate rockets within seconds, followed by a sharp drop in blood pressure, then faintness or semiconsciousness.

This allergy developed in my late thirties when, after drinking a glass of wine, I passed out with an attack of tachy-cardia – an excessively high heart rate. Having done a medical course as part of my podiatry training, I knew the risks of tachycardia, including heart or brain damage due to lack of blood supply, and have avoided alcohol ever since. Even so, since then I have had serious reactions even after carefully explaining the problem, owing to a trace of alcohol left on a serving spoon or because the chef believed that cooking destroys all alcohol – it doesn't.

I borrowed a Japanese cookery book and discovered to my horror that most of the recipes included sake, the strong rice wine, especially in sauces. That could mean spending the whole of any trip to Japan eating at Western takeaways! But there must surely be simpler food available. I borrowed a Japanese dictionary and copied the Japanese words for allergy and alcohol (*arerugii* and *arukoru*). I realised that this would still not be enough to make people understand the severity of the problem, that to me alcohol in any quan-tity, even cooked, is a dangerous poison. Nor did it take the project any further forward. But at least I was armed with some vital information.

During August I had some encouragement – not from the outside, but through a kind of inner voice that has helped me from time to time. Sometimes I 'sense' a word or phrase, which is repeated over and over again. Because it is on the edge of my awareness, it is the persistent repetition that eventually draws my attention to it. It has an insistent quality that demands a response – if it relates to someone I am with at the time I have to say something, because the words will keep on going round in my head until I do. It can feel a bit odd, though it is not unpleasant.

It could be that the words come from a spirit guide, from the collective unconscious or my own unconscious mind. I do not question the source too much; what I know is that when this happens it usually means something. Earlier in the year, in January, I kept sensing the words, 'Be ready to catch the ball.' At the same time I saw, rushing towards me, a shape like a bright, shining ball. At that time I had not thought even about starting on my Japan project. I wrote the phrase down on a piece of sunshine-yellow card and taped it to a shelf above my desk as a reminder. It seemed like a clue to whatever was going to happen during the forthcoming period of change.

Now I kept sensing the word 'October', which repeated itself over and over until I wrote it down. At first I wondered if this related to the seventieth anniversary of Mary Sutton's death, which would be in October. But then I kept hearing, or rather sensing, the number 9. If this referred to a date, 9 October had no significance for me. I wrote both 'October' and '9' on the yellow card. It was not long before everyone I knew had heard about my expectation of some-thing happening in October – to the point where they were probably bored with it, but would at least remember it. The last time I had a persistent precognition of a date it was of

A photo of St Andrew's Church, Malahide.

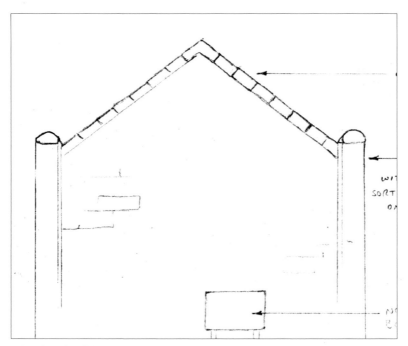

The sketch of the church at Malahide drawn under hypnosis, which I gave to Colin Skinner.

Mary Sutton with daughter Phyllis, aged 2, in 1927.

The Rotunda Maternity Hospital in Dublin. In the presence of a film crew I visited the hospital and managed to locate the small isolation room in which I vividly remembered Mary dying in 1932.

With Mary's eldest child, Sonny, at our first meeting in September 1990.

The four brothers when first reunited in 1985. From the left: John, Christy, Frank and Sonny.

The jetty, Malahide, where I remember standing at dusk, waiting for a boat to return.

Sonny and I visit the film set for *Yesterday's Children* with Jane Seymour and Hume Cronin.

Sonny and me in 2000.

Postcard of the Japanese hotel on Iwaya Toumi no Hana from the air.

September 1999; for two years, I kept writing September 1999 on cheques by mistake. In September 1999 I was made redundant from my part-time health authority job after twenty-five years.

The interview for *Horizon* reached the stage of initial planning and telephone discussions. During these conversations I was reminded how much past lives can affect everything we do and much of who we are. On two days running I had cut the researcher short on the telephone, saying that it was time for me to cook. When he contacted my mother to request an interview, she explained that I had to prepare meals on time because as Mary Sutton I would risk a beating if the food was not ready when my husband wanted it. Although I had come to terms with that life, this had become a habit that I was not aware of until my mother pointed it out.

It was also my past life as Mary that would drive me to clean all the curtains and carpets in August. This was the time of year when, as Mary, I had to refill the mattresses with chaff after harvest, and the smell of ripe wheat was a trigger. This particular August I had already painted the exterior of the cottage, washed all the curtains and bedding, and shampooed the carpets.

When the planned interview came about, my need to do things properly and answer questions concisely overrode my desire to talk about Japan, and in the end I made only a slight reference to it. I continued to ask for help whenever I could find a possible source, such as the *Mensa International Journal* – perhaps they knew of someone in Kitakyūshū who could research local records for me. Then I thought of posting a similar request on an Internet site in Japan, which Neil did for me.

Only then did I realise how much I was asking. In the late nineteenth century, Japan was going through a massive modernisation, which meant there could well be newspaper or microfiche archives. Trawling through these would be a huge task, especially with no names available; I couldn't realistically expect anyone to undertake this for me. If it was just a matter of finding the ruins of an old house on the coast overlooking a bay to the west of Kitakyūshū, I could do that myself, eventually – though a house made on a wooden frame could have rotted away years ago.

Perhaps someone could ask local people about the history of the families who had lived by the bay. There were obvious problems in researching someone who had died 122 years ago, or more. Coincidentally, I discovered that the oldest person in the world, Kamato Hongo, who would be 115 in September 2002, lived on the island of Kyūshū. But even she was born at least seven years after the death I recall and would be unlikely to know anything even if she had lived nearby. The whole venture was beginning to seem impossible.

Nevertheless, I still felt that something would happen in October, and I had been to a travel agency to find out the cost of a trip to Japan. I couldn't afford it at this point, but I assumed that if I was meant to go the means would present themselves. But as October approached I became more and more uneasy. Then, as I was doing the housework one day, a name popped into my head. It was a Japanese name, disyllabic, and there was some ambiguity about the gender: it was either a man's name for a girl or a girl's name for a man. I added it to the yellow card above my desk, and told friends about it for the record.

Things were getting me down. I was tired. Steve's van had broken down and I was driving a round trip of twenty miles to drop him off before going to work myself. My daughter needed lots of errands carried out before she went off to college. As usual, she had left everything till the last minute, so I had to rush around helping her in my rare spare moments. And then there were the rats. Every year when the fields around us are harvested and then ploughed, all the rats and field mice migrate towards the houses. These had never presented a problem, except in the loft, but now I had the unnerving experience of seeing either a huge mouse or a baby rat in an upstairs room. As well as everything else I had to move an ultrasonic deterrent from room to room and put down poison.

The stress was getting to me. October was coming, and I was in no fit state to cope with whatever it would bring. Nevertheless, I continued to drive myself forward. I ordered an English–Japanese dictionary from the bookshop and tried again for a map of Kitakyūshū city. I decided to aim to travel in the spring; there would be no point in waiting any longer for something miraculous to happen. Failing all else, I could borrow the money for the fare. I checked the dates of Japanese national holidays so that my proposed dates would not clash with busy holiday times.

As the reality started to dawn on me, fear added to my stress. The idea of organising such a trip was daunting. We had never had a holiday abroad, and although I had taken many trips to give lectures or interviews in other countries, the arrangements had always been made for me. Most of these trips, even to the USA, had been for only a couple of days and I would usually forgo any fee in exchange for help towards Steve's travel costs so that I did not have to go alone.

There had been no response to any of my enquiries, and I had heard nothing further from the Japanese television company. I felt apprehensive and negative. To make matters worse, an hour or so spent with Neil, who had worked in Japan, highlighted the prospective difficulties. He told me that everything was very expensive – hotels in Tokyo could cost three times as much as those in London, and he had spent £1000 on just three train journeys. Then, when we discussed the problem of arrival at an airport or station where all the signs would be in Japanese, I realised that my ignorance of Japanese would be a severe disability. Worse, Neil confirmed my initial fears about the presence of alcohol in food. Wine, he told me, is used in a great many dishes, including rice dishes; indeed, virtually every Japanese dish that I could find a reference to seemed to contain alcohol.

I was tempted to throw my hands in the air and give up. I could not afford to go, I could not travel around without help, I could not make enquiries without help, I could not eat anything when I got there, and there was no guarantee of success if I did go. The whole idea was a disaster.

Still I could not let go. I trawled through Tesco and found oat cakes, whole-grain crackers and energy bars on which I might be able to survive. Somehow, concentrating on solving the food problem made the project seem feasible after all – forget the escalating costs and language problems, even the fact that I had not been able to check the location properly on a decent map! But I knew that, realistically, I could not undertake the venture without help, and I had no idea how to get help.

The stress was affecting me physically. I keep my back problem in order with lots of cycling, rigorous daily exercises and regular visits to the chiropractor, but now none of this was enough, and I was suffering back and neck pain. I knew that if only I could give up and forget about it, get on with my normal life, the tension would fade away. But I could not give up.

One night I found myself dreaming of a day out with my children to visit a shrine with volcanic hot-water springs. Although it was displaced to my present location and a time when my children were young, it was obviously based on Japan and the past. But I sensed that it could be an omen for the future. Premonitory dreams are often full of symbolic imagery, rather than the realistic form taken by waking premonitions.

I began to ask myself why resolving my past lives had become so important to me that I was willing to pursue the truth of the memories at such personal cost. At one time I had wondered if it was a displacement activity, protecting me from facing up to the conflicts in my present life. But since I had, over the years and in many small steps, resolved many of these conflicts – such as my anger at my father – this was no longer the case. Of course, my aim was for closure – but what did that entail? Was it even necessary to identify my Japanese family?

An answer came as I was cycling. I had a free day for once and decided to fulfil a small ambition by cycling fifty miles on a mountain bike, to make sure I still could. Cycling seems to help my back, and ideas or answers often pop into my head after I have cycled five or six miles and settled into a pace. Now, halfway round, I realised that the reason I needed confirmation of my Japanese life was, at least in part, that I wanted to apologise to the family for letting them down over my marriage. Absurd and impossible though this might be, that was the answer that came into my head.

When I got home I found a telephone message from a freelance coordinator working for the Japanese production company who had visited in April. They wanted to do a follow-up programme and were suggesting I travel to Japan the very next week – possibly on 29 October. Interestingly, when I returned the call, the coordinator told me that his name was abbreviated because it was difficult to say, but that its shortened version was a girl's name. I shall refer to him as Keiko – not his actual name. Keiko told me the production company would cover the costs of my trip and wanted to know what my fee would be. I was shocked to be asked. The trip itself was more than I could hope for. I explained that I do not make television appearances for money.

During our discussions over the next day or so, Keiko brought up the question of hypnosis: his employers in Japan were wondering if I could be hypnotised through a translator, to help me remember more details. I thought this was unlikely – though afterwards I realised that since I go under very easily I might not need a translator until I was already partially hypnotised. I wondered why they wanted to use hypnosis at all, but since I didn't want to jeopardise the trip I thought I had better agree. At the same time, my usual alarm bells were ringing; I knew only too well that it is risky to undergo hypnosis without follow-up, because it can stir up so much.

Keiko was concerned that there would not be enough time to verify the past life, as the proposed schedule was very tight. I suggested that perhaps if they broadcast the details in the programme they might be contacted by someone who remembered the family; if there was a response we could then do a brief follow-up about it. Keiko seemed unsure about this, and I realised that it might work for me but would not be useful for the programme. In a further discussion I said that all we could do was to try to match the location, which was very specific, and then see if it was possible to match a family history to it.

After hypnosis had been suggested to help me remember more, I started to worry whether I remembered enough. Were the location and the brief family history enough? Keiko asked me how I remember. I explained, 'If I ask you to remember your first day at school, you will find that odd images come to mind,' which he understood.

Thinking about this afterwards and realising how simple it was, I found more memories coming to mind. First I remembered sewing the rolled edge of a piece of fabric, and that I was not allowed to use pins – perhaps because the fabric was so fine. Then I found myself thinking about cleaning the house for my mother, and I could see a fan-shaped broom made of bound stems.

The trip was finally planned for 31 October. It was all at far too short notice. There were so many arrangements to make for my patients, my family and myself. I was very nervous: I must not let the television company down; I must try to remember enough for it to be worthwhile; and my memories must be completely accurate, or we might fail to pinpoint the location. In addition, I was a tall, clumsy foreigner claiming to have been an elegant young Japanese girl – would they be able to see her inside this body? I was worrying about too many things at once, and not necessarily the important things.

I looked at the bright yellow card above my desk, and realised how much was falling into place. I had been told to be prepared, and that October would be significant. I had even been told about a cross-gender name, though at this point, the number 9 remained a mystery. I reminded myself that this was to be the last significant period of my life. It was a relief that this time of change was imminent; after the next couple of years I could see my life settling down to a gentler pace. Although I was very excited about going to Japan at last, a part of me was wishing it were all over. Intuitively, I knew that I was in for quite a rough ride.

CHAPTER 10
Going Home

The day before the trip Keiko came round to do some background filming, with a brand-new camera and instructions on how to use it. He turned out to be middle-aged, short and slightly plump. He asked me to talk about my memories, and I tried to detail as much as I could, as accurately as possible. He was easy to get on with, which was a relief as he was also to be my interpreter and minder on the trip – and because of my allergies I would need him to take care of my diet.

He told me that someone from the production company had already been to Kitakyūshū to check out the area of the bay with the peninsula, which was still fairly rural and seemed quite similar to my description. This boded well. We arranged to meet at the airport next morning by the check-in desk, but in my mind I was already in Japan.

Long-haul flights are exhausting. I had to make a very early start for the two-hour drive to the airport, followed by the usual lengthy waiting around. It is hard to sleep on a plane, and I expected to arrive in Tokyo feeling tired after the eleven-hour flight. I was not wrong. When we arrived, I had missed a night because of the nine-hour time difference, and

Sketch map of Japan showing location of the peninsula on Kyūshū Island where I remembered living

two days of my life had run into one very long, disorienting, nightless confusion.

At the airport we were met by Mino, a friendly, attractive young woman researcher from the production company employed by the television company. Mino spoke a little English, and accompanied us to the hotel bus, which took us the forty-one miles into Tokyo. As we travelled through toll roads and over high flyovers we passed many crowded urban areas with dense, high-rise buildings crammed between factories and yet more flyovers – this was modern Japan, not the rural landscape of my memories.

We arrived at the Tokyo Prince Hotel in the early afternoon, where I noted that my room number, 979, was on the ninth floor. (The number 9 was to crop up several times more during my stay. Our flight number had been 900. Most significantly, perhaps, I later learned that Kyūshū means 'nine counties'.) I just had time for a shower before our first meeting with the Nippon TV producer, accompanied by Mino. We had a pleasant discussion about my memories; I described the style of the veranda and Mino made some sketches.

We also talked about a possible family name. This had always eluded me, but each time I tried to recapture it I would imagine a piece of bark or very rough wood, and perhaps a sense of sharpness, which I thought might relate to the meaning of the name. As for my first name, whenever I tried to recall it I would see flowers floating on water. Now the producer, through Keiko, pointed out that wood or bark with sharpness could indicate the name of a tree, such as a pine tree, which has sharp needles. Most Japanese names are apparently linked to natural things such as fields, mountains and often trees.

Something I had to start getting used to was that virtually every statement had to go through Keiko, as translator. I was annoyed with myself for not even attempting some understanding of Japanese before the visit – I also felt that it was impolite on my part. I had known that I would be going to Japan at some point, and could have prepared myself better.

Although everything felt a little odd, the hotel was comfortable and everyone was friendly. But I was bothered by the fact that no one gave me an itinerary or schedule. Researching a past life is disorienting in itself and I would have welcomed some kind of written plan. I had asked Keiko for a schedule before the trip, explaining that I had to know what I was doing, but had been fobbed off with a vague spoken outline. As it was, I had little idea of what was going on and felt progressively out of the loop, although I was supposed to be at its centre. This was the start of several difficulties that I was to find increasingly disturbing. I tried to cope with them without complaint – though, on looking back, I see that a bit of healthy cynicism might actually have been more helpful.

In addition, since I was awed by the generous offer of the trip and was anxious to do my very best, my nerves now brought on a painful bout of irritable bowel syndrome, another stress-related problem that I usually manage to keep in check. Even worse was my fear of an allergic reaction: right from the start I was worrying about what food might be safe, and I gradually became aware that Keiko was not taking my allergies seriously at all. His casual attitude to the dangers meant that throughout the trip I had little safe food and many missed meals. What with jet lag and lack of food over the past twenty-five hours I had been awake, I slept only fitfully that night.

Next day, Keiko announced that he was visiting a friend so I had the morning free. We would meet in the foyer that afternoon. Although I could have done with more sleep I was too keyed up to rest, and I walked out to explore the city on my own. Despite the heavy traffic and dense city development it felt quite safe to be walking about alone. I found a quiet park rising out of the skyscraper jungle, and climbed the many steps to the highest point to get a view of Tokyo;

when I got there I found that the city was obscured by judi-ciously planted greenery, creating a welcome sense of peace. A little later I found a similar tranquillity in the courtyard of a rather magnificent temple, where small birds approached me in the hope of food. Sleep-deprived as I was, everything felt strange and dreamlike.

This was when I made a small but annoying mistake – coincidentally the same mistake I had made on my first trip to Malahide in 1989. I changed the film in my camera and failed to connect the spool securely to the ratchet, so that it didn't wind on. As a result when I got back I had no photo-graphs beyond the first few of the temple and park.

No arrangements had been made for lunch, and I didn't know what I was supposed to do. I was terrified of going into a restaurant, because I had not enough Japanese to ensure that my allergies were properly understood. Rather than take the risk, I settled for one of the energy bars I had brought with me, which was really not enough. I had been so thrown by the time change that I had not eaten – or slept – anything like enough to maintain my blood sugar levels.

That afternoon I was to record an interview at the hotel. We set up in a small, stuffy room, where I was left alone for some time while the crew tried to trace the interviewer, who had gone to the wrong hotel. Suddenly, the room started to go round and I felt cold and shaky. This was not good. I rummaged in my bag for a few glucose tablets and left the room to splash my face in cold water, hoping I would not pass out.

Five minutes later the interview began, and lasted for about an hour. I was so far out of things that I have very little recollection of how it went. I think I managed to remain articulate and conceal the fact that I was unwell, but I felt remote from it all. I was shown a map that I had not seen before and had difficulty locating the right bay; inside I was feeling disoriented and panicky, just when I should have had all my senses about me. Here was my very first opportunity to take a good look at a map that showed the coastline in detail – the map I had been seeking for so long. And I could barely focus on it.

I would have liked to sit quietly with the map and let deeper memories and psychic insight take over. But, the interview over, the map was folded up and removed, and my chances of learning anything from it disappeared. I was puzzled – the sensible thing would have been for the production team to send me some maps of the peninsula several weeks before the trip; doing it this way was unnecessarily hard. Why was I not allowed to look at the map properly now?

However, more immediately, my light-headedness demanded attention. After the interview, Keiko took me for a coffee and I ordered some ham sandwiches, which I couldn't finish, despite my hunger. Perhaps I should have told Keiko how I was feeling, but I really didn't want to complain. At 5.30 I had to meet the film crew in the lobby, as we were going to see the hypnotist. Despite my reservations, I felt under an obligation to the programmers to justify the expense of bringing me over, and it seemed only polite to do whatever I could to make things easier for them. I am often overeager to get things right when I am nervous, but during my time in Japan I took this to extremes. It was as if the well-brought-up Japanese girl I had once been had come to the fore of my consciousness and my behaviour.

The car containing me, Keiko, Mino, a cameraman and

soundman crawled through a maze of narrow streets towards the residential area. As Keiko remarked, 'It is difficult to find addresses in Japan.' Finally we arrived at a small apartment block. The hypnotist, to my relief, was a delightful young woman with whom I felt immediately at ease. Setting up, as always, took some time, but eventually I was lying down in my usual meditation position. I was given headphones that provided white noise and subtle sounds to help the relaxation process. In fact I was so tired that it was difficult to stay awake.

To my great surprise, when the hypnotist began to speak, interpreted by Keiko, it worked: hypnosis via an interpreter is actually possible, though the headphone sounds made the process easier. Keiko turned out to be very competent at translating the context as well as the meaning of the hypnotist's words.

Unfortunately, I had omitted my usual warning when being hypnotised, not to be taken back to my early childhood. This is common practice at the start of a regression but I had somehow assumed that I would be taken directly to my Japanese life. To my horror I returned to one of the worst times of my childhood. Already deeply under, I was unable to avoid it, and the film crew ended up with a lot of tape of me going through some embarrassing emotional outbursts, which I would dearly have wished to avoid. Hypnosis tends to strip away one's façade of self-control, and this may have been exacerbated by the fact that I had all day been trying to conceal my stress and carry on with some dignity.

I managed to regain my self-control and, taken at last to my Japanese life, I duly described the images that arose, none of which were especially different from my previous memories

– or any more useful. However, I did gain a slightly altered perspective on events.

Remembering being a child in Japan, I experienced a kind of childish innocence that I have never really known in my current life, and a sense of wonder at the simple things in life. It was heartening, especially after my disturbing start. I found myself looking again at the mountains that bordered the horizon, and then out to sea across the bay. I could see the nearby houses and members of my family, all already familiar to me. I was asked about names, with the usual negative results; part of the problem was that the memory was now implanted in my English brain, which did not know any Japanese.

At several points I was unable to understand what was being said – despite many years in London, Keiko had never quite mastered English vowel sounds. At these moments I remained silent, too deeply hypnotised to speak. Then, however, something interesting happened, which I was told about only afterwards. Asked in Japanese about the colour of my hair, I answered the question *before* it was translated.

Shortly afterwards, my memory spontaneously leaped forward to the day of the boat accident, but I baulked at reliving the accident itself. Realising this, the hypnotist gently coaxed me through it, and as she did so I had a new and healing insight about my death. I had always felt guilty that the drowning that saved me from an unwanted marriage may have been semi-intentional. Now, under hypnosis, I discovered that, by that point, the young girl I had been was prepared to go through this major life change, to marry and leave home. In fact, the actual change brought about by drowning – the transition to death – was one she was not ready for. Now I realised that the accident had been just that: a complete accident. Instead of guilt I experienced at first anger, then sadness. The guilt simply faded away.

I awoke feeling exposed and vulnerable. I would have liked to return to the hotel and rest, but the hypnotist had to give further interviews. Our return trip included stopping off at the production office, which was tucked away in an area of narrow streets. I was surprised to find people still at work so late. When at last we got back to the hotel by taxi, it was after midnight.

Throughout this long evening, no food was provided. By now I was too tired to worry about eating, and hoped at least for sleep, but could manage only a few hours. I function best on nine hours' sleep, and had had less than nine in all since leaving home on 31 October. Next day, 3 November, we had to be up by 5.15 to catch a plane south to Kyūshū island.

As I prepared for bed, the lack of food and sleep made me think of ascetics who practise abstinence in order to achieve enlightenment. This is not a course I would willingly choose, but as I was on a quest of some personal spiritual importance, the connection seemed oddly appropriate. Unfortunately, my own process seemed unlikely to end in enlightenment.

Next morning, I set out feeling decidedly more cheerful, blissfully unaware that this would turn out to be the worst day of the whole trip. Five of us travelled on an internal flight from Haneda (Tokyo International) Airport, including the cameraman, Keiko, Mino and another young woman researcher. As we approached our destination, the clouds cleared and from my window seat I saw a rocky peninsula and sweeping bay. It was a brief glimpse, but it looked so right I felt encouraged – I could not wait to arrive.

However, when we disembarked at Fukuoka Airport the atmosphere around me changed. Something odd was going on. The two women seemed slightly distracted – there was a shuffling of feet, averted gazes, and a sense of embarrassment. It was unsettling.

The sound man met us outside the airport and after loading up the kind of people carrier favoured by film crews, he drove us north towards the city of Kitakyūshū. From time to time we passed near the coast, and I asked if we were going directly to the bay. Keiko said, 'I do not know.' No further information was offered and Keiko's evasiveness left me feeling disconcerted. Something was not right.

After leaving the town and winding a little inland, we drove past several large lakes that suddenly looked very familiar. But the familiarity was not from any past-life memory: more ominously, this place had appeared some time before in a disturbing dream. A cold, clammy feeling came over me. I turned to Keiko and said, 'I've dreamed about this area. In my dream I passed these lakes and panicked because I did not recognise anything, and for some reason I was supposed to.' As I realised what I'd just said, my stomach started to do somersaults. Keiko, apparently preoccupied with his own agenda, did not pursue the subject.

Quite soon we pulled into a side road lined with wind-blown pine trees, and made our way towards a small bay. It was clearly not the bay of my memories or descriptions. The camera was rolling and Keiko was asking me puzzling questions, such as what did I think about the trees? I didn't know why he was asking, or what sort of answers he wanted. Everything felt surreal. Images from the dream pursued me, adding to my growing sense of confusion. If the dream had been meant as a warning, there was still no escape from what felt like impending disaster.

This was only the first of several wrong locations I was taken to. Much later I realised that this was a deliberate piece of subterfuge, which would account for the edginess I had sensed in my companions. Perhaps they thought that testing me in this way would make good television, but it was making everyone feel uncomfortable. As an indication of the amount of trust the TV company had in my abilities, it could have been either flattering or scary, or it could simply indicate scepticism. Whatever the cause, or mixture of causes, it worked badly for me. As I answered questions in what I hoped was a controlled manner, I was beginning to fall apart, in a very internalised and very quiet way. I was more stressed and anxious than I could ever recall being before.

I looked out to a misty sea, breathing in the fresh air and trying to regain some composure. It was easy enough to say that this was the wrong bay and walk away from it, but by the time we got back to the vehicle I was feeling thoroughly insecure. Around me the crew were talking in Japanese, presumably discussing their next move. I felt excluded, and was concealing an ever-growing anger, but I fought to keep calm. I was still feeling very peculiar from jet lag, and lack of sleep and food, but the psychological pressure of being kept in the dark was becoming unbearable. I could not function like this; my brain seemed to be shutting down. And another reason for my stress occurred to me: I was going back home, but as a foreigner, an outsider. The nearer I came to 'home', the greater became the perceptual gap between who I had been in that past life and who I was now.

We made another stop and got out at another bay. The beach was too long and the peninsula too short and not at all rocky – yet inexplicably the crew encouraged me to think we were at the right place. Sheer panic took over as I charged off with no conscious motivation, and did not stop my brisk escape until halfway along the beach. Beside me, Keiko was asking me apparently irrelevant questions, which reinforced the sense of duality. I felt I was fighting a defensive position in a war I had not started. Finally, I took out a compass I had brought with me, which confirmed that the bay was facing in the wrong direction. It was a highly bizarre moment.

By the time we got to the next stop I no longer wanted to play games; I didn't even want to get out of the car. But, confused as I was, I was still desperately trying to remain polite and helpful. This time we were at a large fishing village where lots of boats were moored. I had no idea why we had come here. The reason became apparent when I was asked if I could identify the kind of boat I remembered crossing in. We had not come to look at the bay but at the boats. I wished someone had told me beforehand: it would have been so much easier to concentrate. Reminding myself that I was here to do a programme and that my own goals were secondary to the task, I got out of the car and managed to find a boat that looked similar to the one I remembered.

By assuming that we were going to 'my' bay, I had set myself up for disappointment. What amounted to 120 odd years of separation angst was catching up with me. I felt like a child who has been promised a trip to Disneyland and finds itself at the dentist's.

CHAPTER 11
Kitakyūshū

Lunch that day was the first proper meal I had eaten since leaving home, three and a half days before. We stopped at a traditional restaurant, where for the first time I experienced – and enjoyed – Japanese cooking. We ate tempura (battered vegetables and fish) served with rice and misoshiru (bean soup). I thought it best not to touch the dipping sauce for the tempura even though I was told that it was alcohol-free. (For once my judgement was good: some eighteen months later I was looking at oriental recipes and found that all those for tempura dipping sauce contained alcohol.)

In the afternoon I was subdued; I was no longer desperately hungry and my head was clearing, but my stomach cramps and disorientation continued. I was still being told nothing, but found I could cope with this better by mentally switching off. It was when we finally arrived in Kitakyūshū city that I began to realise we were still not going to the bay. We pulled up at the new Museum of Natural History and Human History, which had opened only the day before. As it was also the Sunday of a holiday weekend (Culture Day), it was quite busy and we took some time finding somewhere to park.

I was now told that an interview had been arranged with a museum historian, which was of course all in Japanese. Although I was theoretically involved, I managed to get in only one question, and ascertained that until after the turn of the century the roads out of the town were just tracks. After that, feeling I was in the way, I melted into the background while the filming continued.

Afterwards I found the strength to insist on being given some feedback about the interview. Keiko told me that the discussion had centred on the location, and the father's possible employment. The historian thought that he could have been the equivalent of a local councillor, as I had described him as 'a manager of people'. Also, he had found people in the area with the family name of Pinetree, and agreed with my description of the type of boat used as a ferry – though he commented that the boat in a picture I had picked out was too small for the trip to the mainland.

This, it seemed, was all I would be told about an interview that had taken several hours.

When we reached our hotel I was told that everyone was going for dinner at seven o'clock. Although I was very hungry I could not face the idea of spending more time with the crew. I was fearful of being curt or doing the unforgivable by breaking down in tears, so I said that I needed to rest. I did need sleep, but I needed more urgently to work on my attitude. In the solitude of my room I wrote out all my negativity on paper, throwing it away, and resolving to get past it, to be better company and a more useful member of the team tomorrow.

By the morning I was calmer, though it was the calm of resignation. I felt emotionally shut down, clearly not the best frame of mind for achieving a task as delicate as remembering enough from a past life to locate the site of a house. My mood lifted a little when Keiko told me that the crew were aware I was under pressure. He then undermined this encouragement by repeatedly saying, 'I don't think you will find anything.' I did my best to ignore this.

Television always seems to run on a punishing schedule for everyone involved, and that day the work really began. This time we travelled almost directly to the bay I had had in mind from the start and had indicated on the map. Although I realised that we had probably reached the right place at last, I could not work up any enthusiasm; by now I just wanted it all to be over.

We had parked about a couple of hundred yards south of the peninsula. From there the area didn't look completely right, but I thought it best to reserve judgement and keep a cool head. Owing to my switched-off senses, keeping cool was not hard, but that meant that my intuition sank below the surface, and I had to rely on logic – which did not serve me either. I was too tired to realise that our position did not match my own sketches or descriptions, and that we should be heading for the peninsula – although, somewhere inside me, I knew that was where the house had stood.

Logically, there was a great deal that did look right, such as the location of the island relative to the bay; it was also much the same shape and height that I remembered. The size and angle of the peninsula seemed about right, though the colour of the rock bothered me – it was very light. And there were other problems here, too.

First, there was a coast road, which was unexpected – I later learned it had been constructed in the 1920s.

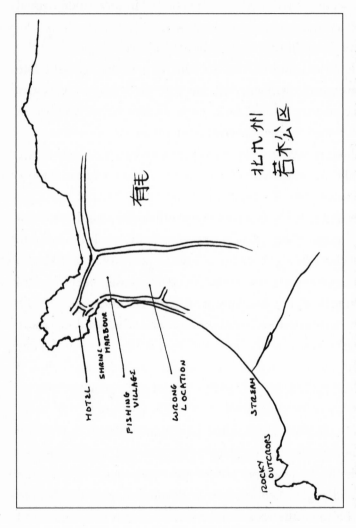

Map of the bay and peninsula showing the hotel where we stayed, and wrong location where we parked

Followed by the crew, I walked along this road towards the peninsula trying to relax enough to think, and was constantly interrupted by reasonable but distracting questions. In the end I gave up and wandered back to the nearest high point close to the vehicle – for no good reason, except that it was at the same height as the site of the house. It didn't look as if there had ever been a house here, and the view from the bay was wrong. I was beyond panic now; I just felt a little concerned. It would be a shame to have come all this way and not get things completely right.

Mino's co-researcher – who I realised was a sceptic – asked me if I thought I had found my home. Her question made me aware of the inner voice that I had been struggling to ignore: I knew I had not. As A. A. Milne's character Eeyore once said, 'The wrong answers are the ones you go looking for when the right answer is looking you in the face.' Instead of stopping a minute to remember the details of the location – that the house and fishing village were close to the peninsula beyond the end of the beach, and that my remembered view of the bay was from the peninsula – my sleep-starved mind just felt numb.

The crew then decided to try a road between the hills that they thought might lead to the fishing village of my memories – despite the fact that there was a village very close to the peninsula that was much more likely to be the one I had known. The place we arrived at was too far from the sea to be a fishing village, but when I pointed this out my companions ignored me. Here, however, we all got out and I had to hang around doing nothing while the team interviewed the local people. As always, I was excluded.

We drove back to the bay for a late lunch at the hotel where we would stay that night, which was on the peninsula itself. Keiko, still not really understanding the nature of my allergies, asked what I would like. I ordered a light sandwich, which seemed the safest bet; what arrived was a tiny, half-sized sandwich containing something that looked like coloured cheese, which I removed – I was sure Keiko wouldn't have checked it for colouring. Unfortunately I didn't manage to remove every trace of the cheese and I suffered a mild allergic reaction to the colouring – annatto, which acts as a neurotoxin. For a quarter of an hour I had palpitations and the shakes. Embarrassed, I explained to the others what was happening, and went out for some fresh air. I crouched in the car park, alone, trembling and giddy, waiting for the effects to pass. No one came to see whether I was all right.

After lunch the two researchers continued interviewing some of the older villagers, this time in the fishing village at the foot of the peninsula. I was not included, or told what was said. But I did notice something: these local people had slight facial characteristics that reminded me of my Japanese father.

Later, the sceptical researcher asked me to accompany her on a walk to see what we could find, though I had lost hope of discovering anything useful. Following the footpath along the top of the peninsula, we found a gap in the trees through which it was possible to gain access to a shelf of rock facing into the bay. The rock was too pale; it looked like a kind of sandstone. But, when I walked further out to look over the edge at the sea-lashed rock below, I realised that the rock was black when wet – exactly as I had mentioned in my descriptions before setting out for Japan. It was a relief to be right about something.

It was not until the next day, as we waited in the car while the researchers were doing some final interviews, that Keiko told me a little of what had they had learned. It was not guaranteed to encourage me. He seemed tired, and I think was either disbelieving or uncomfortable about the whole project. First, he informed me that people were sceptical about my story. This did not particularly bother me. Although a belief in reincarnation is acceptable in Japan, it is common for people only to pay lip service to the idea. He then told me that in the past people used the beach to travel to Kokura, the town at the near edge of present-day Kitakyūshū, implying that my memory of following an overland path with my father must be wrong. I was puzzled. The journey by beach would have involved crossing a wide inlet, which came in from the Kokura estuary – too wide, I thought, for a bridge – which would mean travelling twice the distance of the inland journey. (The bridge we had driven over to get there was relatively new.)

After my walk with the researcher, we came back past a fishermen's shrine, passing a few houses on the way back to the hotel on the peninsula, and I was able to be alone for an hour or so. It was a relief to have some time to myself, to relax and think. My room overlooked the bay. From my window I took in the panoramic view over the eddying ocean to the island and beyond. Tucked behind the far end of the bay to the southwest, dark distant hills rose in a double hump that had all day long looked hauntingly familiar. I gazed for a long time at those rocky peaks, and began to feel at peace.

It was not until several weeks later that I started to feel confident that I really had found the right bay, and that the house could actually have been located under or near what was now the hotel car park. From here the position of the village below accorded with my memories. But at that time, on that day, such thoughts were stirring only in the deeper reaches of my mind. It would be weeks before the enormity of the missed opportunity would hit me.

Mesmerised by the sun going down over the water, I stood taking photographs, unaware that they would not come out. There was something very comfortable about this view. Briefly, a pair of fish eagles hung in the wind close to the window, their huge wings silhouetted against the deep reds of the sunset reflected on the rocks and the sea. For a long time I stood there, the wild autumnal weather just the other side of the glass, the gusty winds, churning seas and dark, heavy clouds cut by shafts of progressively fading sunlight.

As the sun dropped away and the magic faded, my attention was drawn to the written notices around the walls. Although I found it difficult to remember Japanese words when told them, Japanese writing* had intrigued me ever since my arrival and I had already managed to work out some common signs such as 'Exit'. I had a small page of written vocabulary and a guide to the phonetic symbols and I now spent some time trying to understand the notices in my room. Despite my dyslexia, I have always enjoyed cracking codes, which probably uses a different part of the brain from reading. I managed to deconstruct partial words, then tried to construct others. It was relaxing and quite fun; the chal-

---

* Japanese writing is highly complex. It is composed of thousands of *kanji* symbols, based on Chinese writing, which represent whole words, together with two sets of phonetic symbols: *hiragana*, representing Japanese syllables, e.g. *fu, he, chi, ra, ho*; and *katakana*, which is used for foreign words.

lenge took my mind off my stress and helped me to plan calmly what I would say in my next interview.

I decided to ask someone if I had understood the phonetics correctly. Remembering the black rock I worked out the script for *kuro,* meaning 'black'. I showed it to Keiko as we went into dinner, but he seemed dismissive, so I assumed I had got it wrong, and screwed the paper up with some embarrassment.

The crew had arranged a late dinner, and mine was specially prepared without alcohol. It was a wonderful traditional spread of raw fish and curious, large shellfish – sashimi – served with rice. There was sea urchin and many other specialities, including fish floating in a very tasty sweet dark sauce. My hosts seemed prepared for a negative reaction, but I love fish and thoroughly enjoyed the meal.

I had been given plain rice, and was shocked when Keiko suggested I might try the special rice everyone else was eating, as it had 'only a little alcohol' in it. He had still not understood that this would poison me! I tried yet again to explain that even a trace of alcohol could make me very ill, possibly unconscious, for hours. I had been right to be cautious about what I was eating.

Next morning, 5 November, I was interviewed again, in one of the hotel's traditional-style rooms. I was asked such things as whether I remembered shelves in the house I recalled. I knew by now that futons and other items were stored on shelves behind sliding doors during the day, but all I specifically remembered was that the room looked empty. I wanted to report only what I remembered, not what I had learned from other sources.

After answering a few questions, I thought it was time

to stand up and be counted. I had already rehearsed what I wanted to say, and I now explained where I stood as succinctly as possible. I said that in the light of the lack of evidence about the exact location, I felt there were issues to be addressed. There were some surprised expressions on the faces around me. I continued, posing and then answering my own questions. Did I feel I had lived in Japan? Yes, I had no doubts of it. Had I lived on this island? Yes, this was where I had always, since childhood, believed I would find the location. Had we found the right location? Perhaps not, but I was determined not to give up, and wanted to come back. Clearly, I had got one or two things wrong enough to mislead the TV crew, for which I apologised.

The crew seemed a little baffled, and made no direct response. After their initial surprise they simply asked me further questions. Among these, they wanted to know what my attempt at understanding the structure of the written language was all about. Apparently I had understood the symbol structure correctly after all, and had correctly written the symbols for black, *kuro*.

There was still time that morning to realise that this was the right location, or to check the map for other possibilities – if only I had been allowed to borrow it. I could still have got it right just by thinking clearly for a moment. But there were more pressing demands on the schedule.

First, we went to a location that the historian had suggested as likely to be my bay. Once again, I was not told why we were there. When they asked me if I recognised anything, I just shrugged my shoulders and asked where we were. I could not imagine why the historian had thought this bay anything like my sketch: it was just a wide bowl surrounded by hills and fronted with a harbour full of boats, and it faced in completely the wrong direction.

What I was not ready for was a small personal breakthrough on the next stage in the journey, which was to be a trip on the ferry across the sea from the outskirts of Kitakyūshū to the mainland. I had accepted that there would be no kind of definite confirmation of the location – the strongest clue was the yellow rock that turned black when wet. But I had underestimated the transformative effect of just being in the right place.

We had already discussed the ferry trip, and I had been told that it could be hard to trace records of my accident as there were so many fatalities on that stretch of water. Even though it was only about half a mile wide, it was at one time so notorious for accidents that they stopped bothering to report them. I got the impression that there was an undercurrent that meant that anyone who fell in at the wrong point stood a good chance of being sucked under. This sounded eerily familiar, and it supported my claim that my former persona had drowned in that stretch of water.

My problem now was my terror of boats, and especially of that particular stretch of water. However, the boat turned out to be a large car ferry, and the crew succeeded in getting me on it by simply driving aboard, without giving me time to protest. For my part, I had already let them down, so it seemed better to cope with the fear of the ferry than to let them down any more.

Once on board, we got out of the car and went on deck. Because there were so many new docks, everything looked different, but I felt that we must be in the right place. I led the crew to the right side of the boat but refused to stand at the edge with my back to the water as requested – that was the exact position I had taken on that other ferry so long ago. I placed myself three good paces from the edge and grasped the handrail firmly. Then, about two-thirds of the way across, I talked to camera about the accident. Standing there, in at least roughly the right area, triggered a change in me that I could not have anticipated: I relaxed.

Finally, we returned to the museum to do some filming of the traditional boats on show there. I was reluctant to go in, but the crew persuaded me, and I was glad they did. We took a glass lift to the exhibition floor and had a look around. There was a large boat the same size as the original ferry, and a map of sorts that gave me the chance to ponder over the issue of the location. We also found a reconstruction of a 1950s house that had a veranda at the front looking exactly like the one I had described, though made of wood rather than bamboo. This veranda had a small roof with supports, which also exactly matched my description and sketches, though the roofing material was more recent. Now I realised that the timbers of the floor were a continuation of the floor inside the building.

At the museum, I also saw something that gave me a jolt of recognition. It was a photograph, mounted alongside many others, which showed Kokura, now part of the old town, taken in 1915. I stared at it, transfixed: it took me right back, walking through the narrow streets in my kimono, full of trepidation.

That evening we returned to Tokyo. I was hardly aware of the flight, as my mind was filled with images of the ferry crossing, the house in the museum, and many other images from the trip. It was something of a surprise when Keiko,

Mino and I ended up around ten in the evening at the production company offices rather than returning to the hotel. Even more surprisingly, the producer and the executive producer of the production company were waiting there, at that late hour, to take us out for a meal. This courtesy gave me the chance to thank them again for the realisation of a dream ambition, and to apologise for the incompleteness of the experiment.

During this final meal, I had a conversation with Mino, the member of the crew whom I found the most sympathetic. I had a feeling that she was sensitive, and told her that I thought she could do psychometry. To everyone's surprise, Mino admitted to having had a kind of vision on the ferry: as we passed the spot of the accident, she had seen funeral flowers floating on the water, which had shaken her. Later I linked this image with the first name of my Japanese self. At least a year before, I too had seen flowers on water when trying to recall it.

I was still feeling that the whole thing had been a monumental failure. In reality, the chances of completing the task in such a short time had never been great. I had set my expectations too high, and felt that I should have done better. In retrospect, I can see that nobody would have been able to function well within the curiously conflicting aims of the schedule. The way the trip had been run seemed such a waste of time, and possibly counterproductive: broadcasting the programme before the task was complete could jeopardise any future research.

It was unfortunate that my reliance on maps had not been taken into account beforehand. Presumably I had been sent none in order to keep me in the dark as long as possible – yet if only I could have spent time before the trip with a detailed map I could have pinpointed the exact site and avoided a lot of anguish. It was also frustrating that I had had so little access to other information, or to the very useful people who were interviewed and whom I had really wanted to speak to.

Before we parted company, Keiko told me unhelpfully that he thought I should have kept quiet about the memory until or unless it was proven. This struck me as rather illogical, as the trip had made it abundantly clear that I could never have carried out the task on my own. Risking failure had been the only option, even though the presence of a film crew hungry for a story added enormous pressure – as did the short notice and lack of sufficient groundwork beforehand. During this conversation Keiko surprised me by telling me how much he liked his job as he enjoyed looking after people. I could find no reply to this. (I was even more surprised later when we parted company at the airport, and he gave me a warm, very un-Japanese hug!)

Despite everything, there was one positive change in me that it took me a little while to take fully on board. Although the trip had been so disturbing, facing my anxieties about my death by drowning had somehow freed me from another fear. I had always been very uncomfortable using lifts and I had a fear of heights. Yet I had happily got into the glass lift at the museum, and, in the last hotel we stayed at in Tokyo, I found myself entering another glass lift without trepidation. There I travelled to the seventh floor, standing at the very edge and looking down at the swimming pool in the atrium far below, with no problem. It was strange but wonderful to be able to look down without fear, just appreciating the view. This new freedom has stayed with me ever since.

CHAPTER 12

Tracing the Past

I returned home from Japan utterly depressed, and continued to feel upset and disturbed for some time. I was conflicted: I was extremely grateful to the TV company for their generosity but desperately perplexed about the way the trip had been managed, and annoyed that I had not stood up for myself. I tried to tell myself that the difficulties could be put down to misunderstandings, but inside I felt beaten.

In some ways, I did not completely come home from Japan. It was as though I had left part of myself behind. Researching a past life is a life-changing experience. This had been the case with Malahide, and I should have been prepared for some readjustments. After I had returned home from my whirlwind encounter with the country of my past, everything felt different. My inner world had been stirred up and it was going to take time for everything to settle down again.

I began to question everything about my life, including my own identity – not surprisingly, since my past identity was one of the foundations of my present one, and there had been a major shift in my view of that past self. I had returned to my former home as a foreigner, unable to speak the language and with no genetic link to that past. The effects of this had been apparent in the emotional upset I had felt that – discounting all the other difficulties – had seemed so incongruous and uncontrollable at the time.

For a while I was plagued with nightmares and mood swings as I began to come to terms with the emotional upheaval precipitated by the trip, though I tried not to inflict any of this on my family. At a conscious level I knew it was time to recognise that, when I died in Japan almost 130 years ago, that life had ended; it was impossible to go back and pick it up where it had left off. But visiting Japan had made it clear to me that I had not fully *accepted* that it was ended, even though I was clearly no longer that person. I was mourning the loss of part of myself, part of my past. So long as I kept the memory alive in myself, I was somehow able to keep in touch with that identity, and for some reason my present self needed to keep it alive.

I reminded myself that I had always foreseen that the time between the ages of forty-nine and fifty-four would involve changes, possibly quite dramatic changes. As yet I had no idea what these would bring long-term. Even positive change can be disturbing. I was enjoying the novelty of being able to use glass lifts and look down from heights – at home I kept testing myself by standing at the edge of balconies and looking down, still without fear. My son was quite shocked! However, for some time my sense of dissociation made it hard to return to work and my family life. My allegiances had been challenged, as my Japanese persona, previously largely suppressed, had shot to the surface of my conscious-ness, and I was looking at the world through different eyes. It felt odd and disorienting.

As a child I used to gaze at low, grey clouds, and imagine them as mountains. Now, driving about in the unsettled November weather, I found myself doing this again: looking longingly at low clouds on the horizon and wishing they were mountains. With heart-wrenching insight, I understood what this was about. All my life I had been missing the mountains that fill every skyline of Japan. The desire to return home is a strong driving force in anyone who retains a past-life memory. I did not even have photographs to assuage this curious homesickness for a time long gone, and made a mental note to use fail-safe disposable cameras in future.

In mid-November, after catching up on work and sleep and regaining some weight (I had lost ten pounds during the trip) I started to feel stronger, although still far from normal. I was hoping against hope that somehow I might manage to go back there, and on my return home I had belatedly begun to learn the language, putting in some study every day. Towards the end of the trip I had started to understand and recognise phrases that I heard repeatedly, and I acquired a language tape to help develop my spoken Japanese. In fact, writing the simple syllables was turning out to be an excellent way to remember words. Assisted by a new dictionary, I set about tackling the written language. It was a slow job, and proper sentence construction would be beyond me for a while yet, but it seemed a more effective method of learning than simply listening and repeating.

As I thought about continuing the search I realised that I still did not have a proper map. I phoned Keiko, who promised to send one. I did not expect it to arrive until after the programme had been aired, on 7 December, when I would also be sent a video. This would be a good couple of weeks away.

It was becoming increasingly clear that to complete my task I might have to return to Japan at some stage. Since I could make no progress until the map arrived, I spent as much time as possible concentrating on the language and working out the phrases that would be most useful to me. At the top of the list was, 'I am allergic to alcohol', which I learned very fast!

There were other reasons why I felt driven to learn Japanese. I had been severely jolted by the psychological disquiet and total frustration of being unable to speak what had once been my own language. And never again did I want to be in a position in which I could be kept in the dark about plans that concerned me, as I had been in Japan, particularly on the journey from Fukuoka Airport to Kitakyūshū. That was a situation I struggled for a long time to understand.

My studies also brought me an unexpected bonus: the emergence of some new memories. A friend, struck by my fascination with the written language, asked me why I had started to try to *write* Japanese before learning to speak it. Immediately and instinctively, I replied that, when I was about nine or ten, I was offered the chance of a proper education and took great pride as a girl in becoming literate.

Two quiet weeks went by. My restlessness began to abate to the extent that an unusual calm enveloped me. Every day, I continued practising the language, speaking, writing and trying to learn. Eventually, I recorded my own tapes of sentences that I wanted to learn, rather than the usual tourist phrases about trains and shopping.

My exploration into the language brought me some

new information about Japanese culture from the BBC TV language programmes, which I recorded, as they were broadcast in the middle of the night. From these I learned that women are still very much second-class citizens. For instance, a woman graduate, rather than being offered a first step in management like her male counterpart, will be sent on a course to learn how to serve tea to visitors. Women are also expected to retire from work on marriage, and working wives may be ostracised by their neighbours. Society is slowly evolving – there are fewer arranged marriages, for example – but hearing all this, I began to understand how the Japanese attitude to women may have affected my own treatment, as a woman as well as a foreigner.

In anticipation of receiving the map from the production company, I began finding the words to write a reply, using both sets of phonetic symbols. However, December came and went, and neither the map nor the video arrived.

★　★　★

By late January I was waking up every morning convinced that we had eventually gone to the right bay – 'my' bay – although I still didn't know its name. Now that I felt calmer, the view from the hotel kept coming back to me. So I went over my earliest notes to see how far my description of the location matched the position of the hotel.

The house was one of a group of about four on the peninsula, standing apart from the other houses and furthest out. The hotel was set above the bay on an elevated rocky area a short way along the peninsula, with a few houses nestling in the slightly rugged terrain between it and the village.

Although the village was bigger than I remembered, the houses were still clustered below the peninsula, close to the sea.

From the veranda I remembered seeing the sun setting behind the rocky outcrops at the far end of the bay – exactly the view that had so engrossed me on 4 November from the window of my hotel room. I had described there being no beach where the house stood or at that side of the peninsula; this was the case at 'my' bay, where the beach petered out before the peninsula began. The hotel was possibly built a little closer to the edge than the house had been, and had incredible views overlooking the sea-lashed rocks. I had described hills creating a backdrop to the horizon – these must have been the very peaks that looked so familiar as I watched the sun go down. If only I had had the confidence or presence of mind at the time to acknowledge that recognition!

Now I began to wonder again what had been said in the interviews with the local people. I had been told so little – I must try to find out more about the questions that had been asked. What I wanted to ascertain was whether any of the elderly residents had been asked if they knew of a local family who had lost a daughter on the ferry crossing in their grandparents' time. And, since some of the questioning had taken place in a different village from the one nearest the peninsula, had it related to the right location? I tried to get some answers to these and other questions from members of the TV crew, but got no response.

With advice from a journalist acquaintance, I started searching the Internet for maps, aided by my son, who found some fascinating pictures of the Kitakyūshū docks and the stretch of water covered by the ferry crossing, produced by the Kitakyūshū dockland authority. He also found an atlas of Japan advertised on this website, which I immediately ordered. The prospect of obtaining proper maps restored my sense of self-determination: now I no longer had to wait for a response from Japan.

By February I had all but given up hope of receiving a video of the programme, let alone a map, from the production company. And there was another concern: I was also waiting for them to return an old passport they had borrowed, apparently to prove that I had not been to Japan before. I was certain that it was not legitimate for them to keep it, but reminders sent both by me and by Keiko, now back in London, were fruitless.

There must be someone else I could make enquiries to. By now I could construct sentences in Japanese, though I probably could not translate any reply. As well as the basic *hiragana* and *katakana* phonetic symbols (around forty-one of each), written Japanese uses symbols of Chinese origin, called *kanji,* to denote whole words. Of the forty thousand *kanji* characters, some two thousand characters, called *toyo-kanji*, are used regularly. It is a lot to learn.

I could now translate *hiragana* and *katakana* very slowly, and, although I could write using *kanji* and could recognise a few symbols, it was going to take years before I could translate them with any ease. However, the challenge of writing letters of enquiry inspired me with a new enthusiasm. I was already buying Japanese newspapers to see what I could manage to understand – unsurprisingly, this was not very much.

One evening I succeeded in composing a letter requesting information about the history of the hotel site and the people who had lived there before the hotel was built. My completed letter consisted of a few sentences in English followed by a few in Japanese, properly written and hopefully in correctly structured sentences. I thought it looked very pretty, and hoped that it was readable. I had decided to address it to the hotel manager; although I did not know his name, I assumed that the courtesy of adding 'san' (meaning 'sir' or 'madam') would be sufficiently polite.

On 3 February my atlas arrived and I was able to look at the coastline in much more detail. Even so, the scale was poor with 'my' peninsula only a millimetre long. But I was able to make out bays and peninsulas that looked like those we had visited in error, and the position of the islands helped me to rule out a number of possible sites, since the only place where these were west of the bay was at 'my' bay, in a district named Wakamatsu. 'My' bay was also the only one that gave a view of two very lumpy, sharp-looking hills a little to the southwest, behind the rocky outcrops at the end of the bay.

The place names on the map were given in *kanji*, which helped me to make sense of the hotel information sheet I had brought back with me and find the address. This information sheet was an enjoyable challenge. I knew the characters for 'map' and a few other words, and had guessed from the layout which section described the rooms, meals and other facilities, and which were the hotel name and address. I began translating as much as I could, and got rather carried away. Suddenly, to my delight, I realised that I was beginning to recognise not just *katakana* and *hiragana* but also quite a bit of *kanji*. As I looked at the symbols for items such as fire escapes and meal tariffs I had an uplifting realisation

Dear Sir,
Hoteru no shihainin san

ホテル

Please excuse me for troubling you.
O tesu kakete sumimasen

お手数掛けてすみません

I am interested in history of the area between 1860 and 1875
Rekishi nen 1860- 1875 no kyomi wo sosoru.

歴史年 一千八月六十 一千八月七五 の興味をそそる

Who lived there long before the hotel ?
Hoteru wa zutto mae ni sumai wa dare desuka

ホテル は ずっと 前に すまい は だれ ですか

Do you have a photo of the bay?
Wan no shashin wa arimasuka

湾 の 写真 は ありますか

Can anyone else help?
Hoka no dareka ni tetsudatte desu ka

外の だれか に 手伝てて ですか

Prepaid envelope enclosed for reply
Shiharaizumi no futo wo dofu shimasu

支払い済みの封筒 を 同封します

Thank you
Arigato gozaimashita

有難うごでいました

Jenny Cockell

J. Cockell

Sorry, I've only been learning Japanese for four months
Sumimasen ga Nihongo no yon tsuki wo manabu.

すみませんが 日本語の 四月を 学ぶ

Reproduction of my letter to the hotel manager

that basic literacy in this language might not be completely beyond me, eventually.

I was certainly proficient enough to address my letter in Japanese, correctly giving the town first and the addressee last. Since I had no postcode, I pasted a map on the reverse of the envelope and neatly wrote the symbols for 'peninsula' and 'hotel' with an arrow to mark the spot. Before sealing the envelope, I thought to add an enquiry about pictures or postcards of the bay, and finished the task with a self-addressed envelope and an international reply coupon to cover return postage.

This achievement gave me a wonderful sense of self-sufficiency. Even if it took years, there was now a chance I could complete the search myself, and make my own enquiries. It was just thirteen weeks since I had returned from Japan and started to learn the language, and my progress had won me freedom. I no longer had to wait for replies from the production company. I could make my own plans for myself.

Looking again at the address, my eye was caught by something about the *kanji* symbol for the Kitakyūshū ward in which the bay was located. When I translated it I realised that the name of the ward, Wakamatsu, means 'small pine tree'. Could this be the 'wood with sharpness' I had come up with when trying to recall my family name? Had I instead been remembering the name of an area? I had learned that the place names in Kitakyūshū had been changed after the civil upheaval following the Meiji Restoration, during the period I was researching, so the name Wakamatsu would have been extant at the time. Under hypnosis I had seen a name written as several upright parallel lines with small marks between them, and I kept this in mind while looking at the symbols, but could not yet identify it.

When I was researching my Irish life I received a reply to virtually every enquiry I sent out. Now I was trying to reconcile myself to the fact that this time around would be much more difficult, partly due to the language and the distance, and perhaps also due to the more reserved nature of the Japanese. Nonetheless, I felt impatient as I waited for replies.

It may sound strange, but one thing I am certain about is that we are all supposed to forget the past. It is not actually necessary to remember why we choose to do things the way we do in order to make better choices in the future. So in many ways my preoccupation with the past was not helping me to move forward. But it is unresolved issues that hold people back, and that had prompted my quest for the past since childhood. Now, I desperately wanted to finish it all and move on, but I could not see it happening just yet.

As a last-ditch throw I sent a fax to Japan in both English and Japanese, asking again for the return of my old passport and perhaps a map. A week later, a package arrived, containing the passport and a couple of good road maps of the Kyūshū area. Although the paperwork mentioned a video, no video was enclosed.

At last I had maps, which made it much easier to see which bays we had visited and which were definitely wrong. Although my request for an indication of the bays we went to had been ignored, the map was sufficiently detailed for me to work it out for myself. One of the maps was the one that had been used on the trip. My *kanji* was not quite up to using the index, so it was a matter of flipping through the pages to find the relevant areas of coastline. Looking at this very detailed map reinforced my certainty that the last bay we had visited was the right one.

All this was very cheering. I had been stressed and fragile in Japan, and the most difficult day was unintentionally but unfortunately destructive; it was not surprising I had lost confidence. After all, I had been told, in so many words, that it looked as though I had been wrong about everything, and this negativity had made me lose hope before giving myself a chance to succeed. Now things were looking much more positive. I could be absolutely certain that I had been at the right place; everything matched my original descriptions.

The location of the hotel on the map was very similar to my original location for the house. On a walk from the hotel I had found a footpath alongside the car park with a high footbridge leading to steep paths down to a fisherman's shrine close to the village. The village was to the southeast of the hotel and the view from the hotel was across bare rock towards the sea – rock that I had always described as black when wet, and had now seen for myself. And there was a small stream running into the midpoint of the bay, which I had also mentioned. The bay did indeed have jagged rocks at the far end that edged near to the sunset, and I had recognised the hills behind the house.

The structure of the house that I remembered very accurately matched the mock-up and traditional layouts in the Kitakyūshū museum, as did the rush matting on the floors. According to the historian, the roads outside the city were narrow tracks at the time, just wide enough for a horse. And, despite Keiko's claim that locals used the beach for travel in the 1920s, it would not have been possible to use this route to the old town before the industrial development of the 1900s, when the bridge was likely to have been built.

The boats I picked out at the harbour had been agreed by the historian as correct in style for a ferry in the 1880s. And the only photograph at the museum that looked familiar was of the outskirts of old Kokura. The distance across the narrow strait was right, and there had been many fatal accidents on that stretch of water, making my claim of drowning there quite reasonable.

There were a lot of *kanji* symbols on the map around the peninsula. Perhaps it was time to try to translate some of them and find a name for the area and the village. I was able to find the names of all four hotels around the bay, as well as the 'fisherman's shrine', the lighthouse and bus route. Only one group of symbols looked like a place name, but as yet I could not translate it.

Having succeeded in writing one letter, I now had the bit between my teeth. It occurred to me that the historian at the Kitakyūshū museum would be able to tell me when the bridge was built, and whether it had been there in 1880. I also wanted to know more about education for girls in the nineteenth century: whether girls were literate before 1868 and whether literacy commenced then or a year or so later. This would affect my estimated dates of birth and death, which now looked like 1858 and 1875. I worked out the address of the museum, and composed a letter of enquiry. Beyond these, there were only the big questions! I still needed to trace the family, perhaps find the house, and of course find evidence of a young girl who was drowned in that narrow strait.

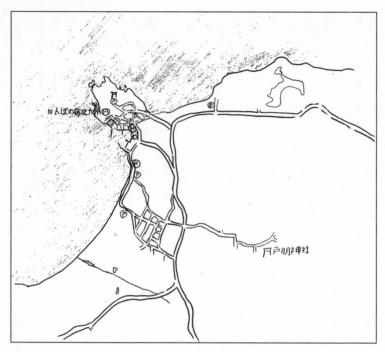

Sketch map of the peninsula showing the location of the hotel and its name written in *kanji*

In March 2003 I was given some information about women's education in Japan by a cycling-club friend who had some Japanese visitors. Much as I had remembered, before 1868 girls were rarely given any education, but with the Meiji Restoration they took a step towards equality when they were included in a scheme for national compulsory education. As well as confirming what I had recalled, this helped to pinpoint the year of my birth as around 1858, since I was about nine when I began learning to read.

For the next few days I considered sending some more enquiries and prepared some more letters, but I had a strong

Dear Sir,
Rekishigakusha san,

歴史学者さん

Please excuse me for troubling you.
O tesu kakete sumimasen

お手数掛けてすみません

I am interested in history of the area between 1860 and 1875
Rekishi nen 1860- 1875 no kyomi wo sosoru.

歴史年一千八百六十一千八百七五の興味をそそる

When was Wakato bridge built?
Wakato hashi wa tateru itsu desu ka

若戸大橋は建てるいつですか

When were all young women literate?
Wakai onna wo zenbu no shikiji wa hajimaru itsu desu ka

若い女を全部の識字わ始まる いつですか

Prepaid envelope enclosed for reply
Shiharaizumi no futo wo dofu shimasu

支払い済みの封筒を同封します

Thank you
Arigato gozaimashita

有難うございました

Jenny Cockell

Jenny Call

Sorry, I've only been learning Japanese for four months
Sumimasen ga Nihongo no yon tsuki wo manabu.

すみませんが日本語の四月を学ぶ

My letter of enquiry to the museum historian in English and Japanese

feeling that I would receive a reply on 18 March, so I waited. In fact, a reply from the hotel manager arrived on the 19th – written in excellent English. He had gone to considerable trouble to find and photocopy some pages from a history of the area where the hotel was built. I did not translate all of these, but learned that the hotel was first built in 1973 on land cleared from farms and coppices; before that all that had stood there was a tower, built around 1730 by a feudal lord as a lookout for smugglers and wrecks.

The cape where the hotel stood was called Iwaya Toumi no Hana. Hana means 'flower', which made me wonder again about names. Further efforts at translation gave me something that, if I had got it right, might be 'Craggy mound, flower on the sea'.

The manager also enclosed two postcards giving aerial views of the hotel (one of which is reproduced in the plate section). They clearly showed the small group of houses near the hotel, raised up from the village and overlooking the bay. The cards also showed quite beautifully how the yellowish rock turns black when wet.

Expressing my very genuine gratitude, I wrote back asking him for further help, mainly in English but with key questions in simple Japanese. I hoped he might be able to direct me to records of some kind. Even if he was unable or unwilling to help me further, someone local might know something.

Meanwhile, I had three double-sized sheets of historical information to translate – an exceedingly slow but enthralling task. I began to piece together what turned out to be a record of the local villages, people and assets, starting much earlier than I needed. After three days I had only roughly translated five lines of the seventy-five lines of script, top to bottom and right to left.

Even though I was still like a child learning to read, the need for literacy was important in a deep psychological sense. One thing I discovered was that the character I had not been able to identify in the hotel name just meant 'lodge'. Soon I found myself reading about Chinese T'ang ships, the watch tower, guard duties, and the Black Field Clan, which seemed to be a

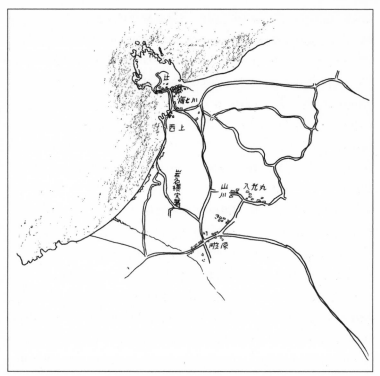

Hand-drawn copy of an old map of the bay

record of smugglers' activities. Along with the historical data was a photocopied map of the peninsula. The hotel was not marked, but the coast road was, so the map dated from somewhere between 1920 and 1979. What drew my attention was a group of houses near the location of the present-day hotel. Could this have included 'my' house? There was a Buddhist temple marked close by and I wondered how long it had been there; I had not seen it on my visit.

Just in case more details were needed I set about preparing a list of relevant points in Japanese, marking what had already been confirmed. It took hours, but it was good practice. Then I prepared an explanatory letter, questions and a list of details, all translated into carefully drawn Japanese characters.

It was heartening to discover that my inner radar was working well. I fell asleep on 13 April expecting to have a letter from the museum in the morning, and woke up early to read it. The letter had indeed arrived: it was from a historian, Mr Hibino of the Kitakyūshū Museum of Natural History and Human History, which I had visited in November. The answers to both my questions were written in beautiful English.

Wakato Bridge was built as late as 1962, and before that the area was cut off from Kitakyūshū by a wide, deep inlet. (This meant that before then it would not have been possible to walk around the beach to reach any of the satellite towns now comprising Kitakyūshū.) There was a very detailed reply to my enquiry about education in Japan. Historically, this varied from place to place and according to social position and gender, but towards the end of the Meiji era the literacy rate of both Japanese men and women had reached almost 100 per cent, owing to the compulsory-education programme.

I decided to write again to the hotel manager, along with a request to pass the details on to anyone who might be able to help. The next step was to write to the historian again asking how I might be able to research the history of a house I had found on the old map sent by the hotel manager. This time, he did not reply.

On 30 May the video of the programme arrived, posted in London, with no label or covering letter. Only part of the programme was about my story and the segment was brief, followed by an audience discussion, which, despite all my studies, I found impossible to follow. Unfortunately, the filmed item did not cover the points confirming my memories, such as the black rock, the ferry crossing and the construction of the house. Rather, it concentrated on one of the locations I had so soon recognised as wrong, but inexplicably excluded the interview in which I *said* it was wrong. Overall, it seemed more detrimental to my case than helpful; simply watching it left me depressed.

June arrived. I now had a reasonable smattering of basic Japanese, but – given all the problems of the previous trip – was no longer so keen to return. Trying to think what else I could do, I made a copy of the 1920s map, which showed the group of houses on the peninsula, and enclosed it in a letter to the Japanese Tourist Board asking if they knew of any records offices to which I could write. I was hoping somehow to trace the family name. They replied suggesting the Kitakyūshū municipal offices (but omitting the address) or a local temple, where records were kept before the war.

Suddenly I realised that I did not need census records to find the family name. The peninsula was an area of low population, and so the name should be easy to find if I asked for records of deaths for the area over a ten-year period, preferably with the age and cause of death – provided, of course, that such records existed.

The temple on the old map had clearly gone, but, looking at the map that the production company had sent, I found another temple fairly nearby in Wakamatsu. I worked out its address using the symbols on the map, and wrote a letter asking for records of deaths for Iwaya Toumi no Hana, writing as usual in English and Japanese – by now the local post office staff were getting used to my letters with pretty *kanji* symbols and supplying international reply coupons.

Since I had no address for the municipal offices, I sent a second letter via the Tourist Office at Kokura Station, asking them to forward it to the records department of the municipal offices. They must have done as I requested, since, early in July, I received a reply from the Kitakyūshū record office. The news was not good. Their oldest records dated back only to 1886. In 1867 the Tokugawa government fell. In 1872 the new government had implemented a new system of births, marriages and deaths, listing family members under the names of the heads of household; however, it was not implemented everywhere at once, and the record office in this area was not functioning until a few years later. The gap between the fall of the previous government and the implementation of the new records system fell neatly into the time period I was researching.

However, the director of the record office had recognised the enclosed historical map as the cover of a book by a local historian, who might be able to help, if I could send further information about my specific line of enquiry. I sent off a brief outline of my research, but did not mention reincarnation – I had no wish to scare him off, particularly as he might be my last chance.

There was no reply to this or any of my other enquiries. For the first time in fifteen months I had no contingency plans. I put away all the paperwork that had been on my desk. I was tired, and unmotivated.

Perhaps it really was time to let go.

CHAPTER 13

The Samurai's Daughter

It was not until the New Year that I began to regain some energy and enthusiasm. In February 2004 I found myself clearing out the study. I threw out the ancient carpet, sanded and stained the floorboards, built extensive storage and shelving, redecorated completely, and reorganised all my paperwork.

Now, despite the earlier lack of response, I considered writing again to the temple asking about other sources of information. Might there have been a census or some collation of causes of death – perhaps reports of ferry accidents? I would need to plan my letter carefully, partly because my Japanese still required simple sentences, and also because experience had taught me that the shorter and simpler the letter, the more likely I was to receive a reply. I delayed composing it for several months.

I needed to find out enough to understand the emotional baggage I was still carrying. My time in Japan had been very strange: it was as though I had been playing a role, trying to suppress my stubborn streak, trying to do as I was asked, quietly, without protest, like the well-brought-up Japanese girl I had once been. But the whole experience of researching the memory in earnest had stirred up a complex array of feelings, just as it had in Ireland, and this time it was taking even longer for the dust to settle. I still felt incomplete; I needed to know more. At the same time I desperately wished I could forget it all and walk away. In fact, for a long time there was little I could do to move on. I still had a busy life with my work and a family who needed my time and attention, and the break helped me to return to my twenty-first-century self.

★ ★ ★

In September 2004 I was heartened by reading about a verified case of past-life memory in the *Fortean Times*, which suggested a broadening tolerance and understanding of reincarnation. A much older memory of my own was revived when I was reading a book about very early history, which mentioned aboriginal women gathering grass seeds to grind between stones. This was something I had done every summer as a child, knowing that it belonged to a very old part of me, but unable to place it. As I read, I realised that the memory was almost certainly of Neolithic times. There is no time limit to past-life recall and it is never too late to feel comforted by finding an answer. As well as reassuring me, it put the furtherance of my research in Japan into perspective. It would never be possible to research and verify all my past lives!

In any case, it now seemed wise to suspend all research, as my health was beginning to suffer – in fact I had not been well since my return. I gradually realised that this was caused by the development of further allergies, and I identified first coffee and then tea as triggers. All my previous allergies had appeared as a result of extreme stress, and had become worse over time. Clearly, now would be a good time to tie up any loose ends and give up. There was one more letter that I planned to tackle, and it should be my last. I finally wrote to the second temple in the area, asking for their assistance. But, although I enclosed the usual international reply coupon and self-addressed envelope, there was no reply.

By 2005, three years after starting the project, I realised it was time to accept that I could do no more. My visit to Japan had shed new light on the story of my death; everything that could be checked had been correct, and I was no longer burdened by guilt. I would still have liked to find objective proof of that past life and death, but without records for the period in question there was no chance of verifying my memories. Inconclusive though my quest was, I must leave it and move on.

Curiously, just as I had made up my mind to let it all go, I received a totally unexpected offer of help, and, by a strange quirk of fate, it came from a Japanese woman. In the spring of 2005 I was contacted by an Irish newspaperman, Hubert Murphy. One of my readers, Hisayo Funakoshi, was so interested in my story that she had visited Ireland to find the sites of Mary Sutton's life; she had approached him, asking to be put in touch with me. She lived in Sri Lanka, and I had been thinking about old friends from Sri Lanka at the time. Partly because I liked this coincidence, partly because it felt right, I was happy for him to pass on my address.

It was some months before a letter arrived from Hisayo, written in excellent English (she also spoke several other languages). We had a lot in common: she was the same age as myself, and a strong believer in reincarnation; she was also very intuitive. She had first heard about me through the TV film of *Yesterday's Children* – coincidentally, this was at the time I began researching my life in Japan. Because the film was targeted at American television, she at first assumed I was American. But one day, travelling by train through North-amptonshire with her student son, she told him she was sure that I lived nearby. When she later read the book, she was surprised to learn that she was quite right.

This letter was the start of an important friendship. From the outset, Hisayo's letters were warm and friendly, and we began writing to each other quite often. She had read my account of my Japanese memory in my second book, *Past Lives, Future Lives* (published in 1996), and now I told her about my recent efforts to trace that life. Hisayo was natu-rally very interested and offered to help me with further research.

Despite my decision to give it all up, Hisayo's support and belief in me renewed my confidence, and I was happy to get started again. I sent her some copies of the paperwork, explaining that it might be impossible to do anything more, as there were no records. Undeterred, she tracked down the official at the Kitakyūshū record office, Mr Inaba, who had answered my enquiry in July 2003. She spoke to him on the telephone at some length, and found him very helpful.

In this letter she corrected a misunderstanding: the name of the peninsula was not Toumi, as I had been told, meaning 'of the sea', but Toomi, meaning 'nose'. (In translation, the use of Western vowels is not consistent, which had caused the confusion.) She also confirmed that records of births and deaths were not kept during the years in question and in any case are not kept in Japan in the way they are here, so the only way to find out about the family would be to ask if anyone remembered them. Since that had already been tried, I was not too hopeful about this.

Hisayo turned out to have the same dogged streak as I did. Later in the year, she actually visited Iwaya Toomi no Hana during a trip home. She stayed at the same hotel, apparently in the very room where I had stayed. And, although she was unable to find any written records, she set about talking to local people, including a girl in the hotel who remembered me, and came up with some new possibilities.

She told me that the Iwaya area had belonged to the Kuroda clan, in the county of Chikuzen. Marriages were arranged within the clan, so the locals thought it unlikely that I would have gone to Kokura, which belonged to the Ogaswara clan. It was even less likely that I would have married someone on the mainland. A much stronger possibility was that my journey had been to Tobata via Wakamatsu town, both homes of the Kuroda clan (and both now absorbed into Kitakyūshū). Wakamatsu town was one side of the wide inlet coming down from the estuary, now crossed by the Wakato Bridge; in the nineteenth century the only way to reach Tobata, on the other side, would have been by ferry.

I was at first resistant to the idea, but on closer examination everything fell into place. I had not taken into account the many changes in the coastline since the nineteenth century. Today, the ferry crossing from Kokura to the mainland has been narrowed by the docks built half a mile on to reclaimed land. In the 1880s it would have been much wider than the crossing I remembered, whereas the channel between

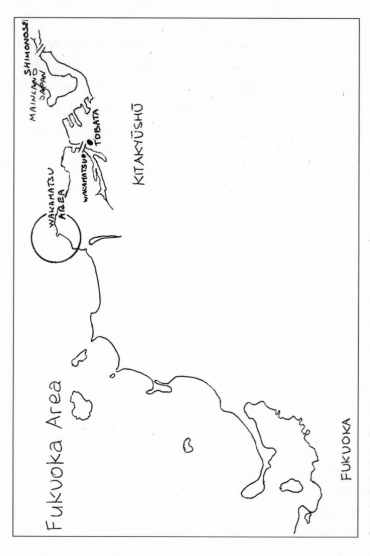

Sketch map of the Fukuoka area of Kyūshū, with the peninsula circled

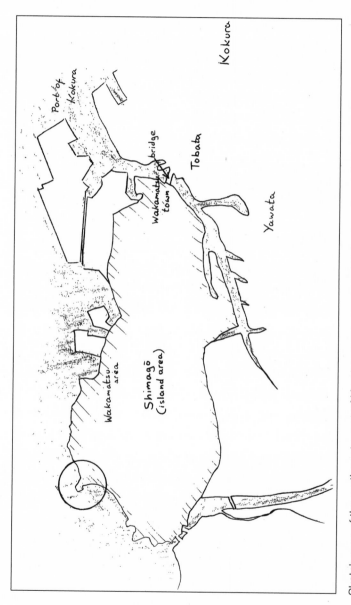

Sketch map of the northwest coast of Kyūshū showing Shimagō (island area) and the bridge which has replaced the ferry crossing

Wakamatsu and Tobata would have been about the right width and would still be subject to tidal undercurrents.

This would explain why the museum historian thought the boat I had picked was too small for the crossing to the mainland. It would also explain why the car ferry did not arrive immediately in a bustling town, as I had expected, whereas the ferry from Wakamatsu would have taken us straight to the busy town of Tobata. As for my recognition of the old photograph of Kokura, the outlying streets of Kokura and Tobata almost certainly merged even then, and the streets in both places would have been very similar.

Hisayo also pointed out that the area on which the peninsula stood was known as Shimagō, meaning 'island area', since it is virtually surrounded by water with the sea to the north and rivers to the east, south and west. This would make sense of my memory of having left one island for another. I had left the 'island area' for what must have seemed to my untravelled self to be another island.

In her search for my family Hisayo had asked a lot of questions, and researched the history of the area. She learned that at the relevant period there were several men of some local importance, including four samurai who watched out for foreign ships. There was also a *shoya*, or village head, who was chosen from and by the farmers. Samurai, who belonged to the order of warrior knights established in feudal Japan, were held in high regard. I remembered my father as being equivalent to middle management, coping with a position 'between people'. This didn't fit with his being a farmer, but suggested that he was one of the four samurai.

Hisayo sent me further information about the history of the area, together with some large-scale modern maps. And she had found a history book that actually gave the names of the four samurai – Hanafusa Seidayū and Shinno Hanjūrō, who were *chigyō* samurai, higher in rank than Hayashi Zenpachi and Takeo Yosaku, who were *ashigaru* samurai.

At the time I thought their names were titles referring to their positions, and did not attempt to translate them. And it was not until I was editing this manuscript in April 2006 that I noticed something on one of Hisayo's maps that made my heart leap. It showed a house in what I can only describe as exactly the right position, almost as far along the peninsula as the hotel and at the top of a rocky escarpment close to the sea with a road sweeping in front of it. This did not prove that a house had been there in the 1870s, but it proved that a house *could* be built there.

In August, when I thought there was nothing else to learn, I suddenly made the connection between the four samurai and the four houses that I remembered on the peninsula. Since there was no reason for anyone other than the samurai attending the watch tower to live out there, it was highly probable that one of them had been my father. This would account for his trips away (to report to Fukuoka), the social separation from the villagers, and the need to arrange a marriage so far from the village. This was exciting!

Now I set to work to translate the samurai's names. The easiest was Hayashi, which means 'woods' – could this relate to my image of bark or rough wood? Shinno, I worked out, means 'new field' – I could disregard this. Takeo had something to do with bamboo, which I could also ignore, as bamboo is smooth and not actually a wood. But Hanafusa might be relevant – Hisayo told me it meant 'a cluster of flowers'. At this point the most likely seemed to be Hayashi,

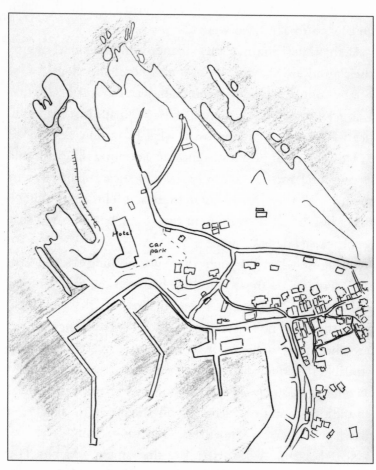

Copy of modern map showing houses on the peninsula

'woods' – especially since the name, represented by a picture of a pair of pine trees, looked very like my earlier recollection of a name written as upright parallel lines enclosing a reversed K.

Now that I had a likely name, perhaps it would be possible to trace some of the samurai's descendants. As I was wondering how to do this, I heard from Hisayo, who had found another contemporary map giving the names of local property owners; she had begun to make enquiries as to whether any of those sharing the two most likely names were actually related to the samurai.

Within a few weeks Hisayo had got in touch with the contacts she had made in the hotel; one of them was a kind woman who was willing to approach some of the families on our behalf. But it turned out that most of the people who shared the family names were not related to the samurai, and their responses were guarded. In typical Japanese manner they were reluctant to discuss family matters, but they may not in any case have known of their family history in the Meiji Restoration period. Since it was so difficult to get a response anyway, Hisayo and I agreed that there was nothing to lose now by explaining to the next people she approached exactly why we wanted the information. She would tell them the whole truth, even if that prevented some people from cooperating.

Later that month Hisayo sent me a translated transcript of the Japanese television programme. Generally, it presented a picture of a satisfactorily completed task, despite its inaccuracies. These no longer concerned me. What did interest me, though, was that the interviewees included an elderly relative of the samurai Hanafusa Seidayū. Hisayo had already begun to think that he was a more likely candidate for the father as Hayashi's rank of *ashigaru* was relatively low – they were usually farmers, given some samurai duties. Hisayo felt strongly that my description of the father and his duties were much more in keeping with a *chigyō* samurai. This idea was strengthened when Hisayo sent me some pictures of historical dress and hairstyles. I compared these with my recollection of my Japanese father in the 1870s, and the styles I picked out were of the correct period.

In November, Hisayo returned to Japan to see her parents and included a visit to Iwaya Toomi no Hana. She was determined to speak to relatives of Hanafusa if she possibly could, as well as trying to trace relatives of the other three samurai. In fact, she did rather well. She managed to locate and spend some time with descendants of the samurai Hanafusa, who showed her a great deal of historical material, including letters and items predating the Meiji Restoration. However, there were gaps in the family records, and the temple that had once been there had been destroyed by fire, which meant that any records it had held had been completely lost.

It struck me as ironic that the period I was trying to research coincided exactly with the civil war, when records were not kept, while any pre-existing records would have disappeared in the temple fire. There were also gaps in some of the family records, due to damage. In addition the samurai families unfortunately suffered very high losses during the Second World War, making it even harder to find out more about family histories. There were few people left to ask, and less oral history would have been handed down. Given all the gaps in information, there seemed no way of confirming the existence of a daughter who drowned at seventeen.

However, Hisayo was then put in touch with a Miss X, a lady who had a very interesting story. She told Hisayo that it was common for samurai to marry their daughters to older men in good positions; several members of the Hanafusa family had married into her own family in this way. And about 150 years ago a girl from this family was to marry an older man in her family, but drowned at the age of seventeen. Had we traced my own story at last? Hisayo was very excited, but there was no way of confirming the story, and it seemed disappointingly vague. It was tantalising; this could very well have been what I was looking for, but without some corroboration I could never be absolutely certain.

Just after Christmas Hisayo telephoned, very pleased: with Miss X as a go-between, the Hanafusa family had given her permission to search through their records. They were written in a very old-fashioned script, which was hard to read, and the year numbering was different from ours, which slowed things down. But at last Hisayo had them in order. It emerged that Hanafusa Seidayū had one daughter and four sons – but, although the daughter was born at about the right time, she survived past 1891. So this was not the right family.

However, the Hanafusa family had owned most of the peninsula, certainly the land on which 'my' house had stood. Hisayo advised me that the family I remembered was likely to have been related: possibly 'my' father was a younger brother of the samurai named in the history book. The land was no longer owned by the family, however. When the samurai class was abolished during the Meiji Restoration it was common for the families to sell their property in order to survive.

Finally, Hisayo visited the descendants of Hanafusa Seidayū – the gentleman who had been interviewed for the TV programme, his wife and his elderly mother – and was delighted to find them very open and friendly. She showed them copies of my books, a copy of the TV film of *Yesterday's Children*, and her research file, and had no problems explaining the rather odd reasons for her visit and the sort of information she was looking for.

She asked them about the questions put by the TV crew, and was surprised to learn that their first and main question was whether any foreigner had lived in the area – to which the answer was 'no'. This made no sense; it made me wonder if the television crew had completely misunderstood what we were looking for.

Hisayo still felt confident that in my past life I had been related to the samurai Hanafusa, but it was going to be extremely difficult to find the records of a brother, or possibly cousin. Miss X was related to the other *chigyō* samurai, Shinno (or Niino) Hanjūrō, and was checking her own family records; she agreed to look out for clues. Hisayo also managed to trace some other families who might be related to the samurai Hanafusa, in the hope of finding out more about their relevant family trees.

It bothered me that Hisayo was doing a great deal of work and enlisting quite a lot of local help, when only a few months earlier I myself had been willing to give up. After all her hard work, I hoped her efforts would yield results, for her peace of mind as much as my own. She had become almost as obsessed by the search as myself.

★　★　★

At the end of January 2007 Hisayo gave me more news. First, the relatives of the *ashigaru* samurai, Hayashi Zenpachi, had kindly provided her with records, which included details of a nineteen-year-old daughter who drowned in 1874. It was a coincidence, but she was already married at the time.

Helpfully, Hisayo had also managed to find another history book, which mentioned that in 1862 a different member of the Hanafusa family was a samurai on the peninsula at the time in question. This was very interesting. Hisayo proposed to make efforts to trace the family tree of a brother of Hanafusa.

Much more importantly, Hisayo had news of the house on the peninsula. When I first told her about it she felt sure my memory was wrong, as from her enquiries and the maps she had seen she was certain that there had never been a house between the cliff and the road. I was insistent that it was one of the most important details: the house was right at the cliff edge with a veranda at the back and a road in front. This was pivotal to all my memories, yet all the houses on the old map seemed to be placed on the other side of the road. Now Hisayo had definite proof that my house had existed!

On a further visit to the Hanafusa family, she had given them a description of the house, based on my information and drawings. They looked at her in astonishment, and said, 'How did you know about that house?' They could actually remember it. It was a second house belonging to the family of Hanafusa Seidayū; it was likely that the head of the family had lived in the main residence, while the younger brother we were looking for would have had the second house.

Both houses had been demolished many years ago now, but

the Hanafusas confirmed that this second house had been very close to the cliff edge, and the family preferred to use it in hot weather, as it was cooled by the breezes from the sea. The position of the house, the layout and its relationship to the path exactly matched my memory of the home I lived in for seventeen years. They told Hisayo how the veranda doors would be left open on hot days to allow the sea breezes to blow through the house.

Hisayo gave me all this information on the telephone, almost speechless with excitement as she confirmed that the house had been exactly as I had described it. She was amazed that I had remembered so many details. At last, we had really good evidence that my memories were accurate.

At Easter 2007 I met Hisayo in Nottingham, where her son and my daughter were both in their final year of university. It was wonderful to meet her at last. She was tiny, but had a presence that made up for her stature, and her whole face was filled by her smile. We had lunch together at a vegetarian restaurant that served European, Oriental and Asian meals, so all four of us enjoyed our favourite dishes.

After lunch my daughter took us to a quiet park where we talked until Hisayo had catch her train. Before leaving, she handed me a sheaf of papers, the fruit of her research into the samurai families mentioned in the history books. During our conversation, it became apparent that it might not be possible to finish the task completely. The samurai Hanafusa had a number of relatives, and it was almost impossible to discover which one had lived in the house by the cliff in the 1870s.

The family that had been so helpful unfortunately did not belong to the right branch. The personal name of the

Hanafusa named in the history book as taking over the task of samurai was indecipherable in the records. Hisayo showed me the papers, explaining that she could not decode the very old-fashioned handwriting. The family name was clear; and he could have been a brother of the samurai Hanafusa, but without his full name it would be impossible to trace any present descendants. And, after the abolition of the samurai class during the Meiji Restoration, there was no way of knowing which member of the family took over the guarding of the peninsula.

A further problem in Hisayo's research was that in Japan only family members may legally research old records. Hisayo and Miss X had gained special permission to do this, but not every branch of the family would allow such prying into their personal history and several surviving relatives had, quite understandably, refused to help. In addition, the branch of the family I needed to trace may not have survived at all, given the losses during the war, and any records of them could well have disappeared altogether.

Almost a year later, at Easter 2008, I was just finishing this book when Hisayo unexpectedly came up with some more information. The great-grandson of the samurai Hanafusa Seidayū and his wife had been in contact again. Since so generously sharing information with Hisayo about their family history, they had expressed an interest in trying to discover my identity in my previous life; Mrs Hanafusa was particularly keen to try to find 'Jenny's family'. I was very moved by their kindness and support. What was more, some other members of the family had started to take an interest. Not only did they want to find out more about their own history, but they were now willing to share this private family information.

So far, all the Hanafusas had been able to do was to fill in the gaps relating to the descendants of Hanafusa Seidayū. They had now found details of his children, with most of their names and birthdates, which ranged through the 1860s and 1870s. Since I was looking at a birthdate in the late 1850s, the father I remember could easily have been a brother of Hanafusa Seidayū – perhaps an older brother starting his family a few years earlier.

Sadly, none of the records contained details of Hanafusa Seidayū's brothers or their descendants. But there is still some hope. A branch of the family descended from his second son moved to Tokyo many years ago; if they can be traced, there is a possibility that they may have records of the samurai's brothers that could lead to finding out the names of his children. As yet, this remains just a possibility.

Nevertheless, we have come a long way. I can be quite certain that I had found the right location, and I was right about the four families living on the peninsula. Of particular relevance, I was totally accurate in my assertion that I was first allowed to learn to read and write at the age of nine, at exactly the time when education became mandatory for all children, including girls.

Finally, and crucially, Hisayo had been able to confirm that the house I remembered, with its veranda at the back overlooking the sea, had existed exactly as I had described it. It had been owned by one of four samurai, confirming the status of the family. I had indicated the correct clothing for the class of family at that time in history. Even the family name had a connection with my image of flowers.

This was probably as far as we would get. But it was a good deal. I could be fairly sure I had found the right family, and that I had been the daughter of a samurai, even though I might never know the name of the girl who drowned at seventeen, or discover more about her father. It would be wonderful if one day the final pieces of the jigsaw were to fall into place, and that somehow I discovered the last few details – but I had learned enough to be satisfied.

Hisayo came to my rescue at a time when I was ready to give up. What she found out through her meticulous research brought a conclusion to the journey I had set out on five years earlier. We may not have found all of the answers, but my main concern had always been to find a resolution and to be able to move on. Now, thanks to Hisayo and the kindness of others, I felt that this was at last possible.

The process of healing became apparent when I revisited the way I felt about my life in Japan. When I started this research I felt I had let down my Japanese father and had a need to apologise to the family. (I did write to their descendants to thank them for their kindness.) Now I realised that something had changed. I remembered that my sense of guilt dying as Mary in Ireland and leaving the children behind was repaired after visiting the Rotunda hospital, facing the reality of the illness and accepting that the death was not my fault. Now I knew that the sense of guilt about dying before my marriage was equally unnecessary: it was not my fault.

My presentiment of an unsettled time between the ages of forty-nine and fifty-four had been only too accurate; my quest had inevitably entailed an emotional roller-coaster ride. Now that time was coming to an end, and I found myself looking forward to a life less disturbed by the past. Now, at last, I could enjoy living in the present. And now, when I recall the view from my Japanese home, looking out to sea from a veranda teetering on a cliff edge, enjoying the cool breeze from the sea in my hair, I can do so without nostalgia, but with gratitude that I was given the chance to see that view again.

CHAPTER 14

Looking at the Future

When I resolved my life as Mary in 1990 I was almost thirty-seven, Mary's age when she died. Just as I had foreseen at the age of sixteen, after a period of change and upheaval, I had come to the end of that part of my life where crushing difficulties and depression were the norm, and the beginning of a new phase in which growth could take place. Free of the burden of all that research, I could now embark on writing a second book – in some ways the book I had always wanted to write. I wanted to convey a sense of the continuity of lives, past, present and future, and I now set out to do this in what became *Past Lives, Future Lives*.

I had always kept notes – somewhat obsessively – of all my psychic experiences, so I had a good deal of material about my other past lives, and also of a number of premonitions in the form of dreams or waking glimpses of the future. These precognitive experiences always have the same quality as the memory of an event that has already happened. Rather than seeing a future that has not yet happened, I feel as if I am picking up an event that has already been set in time.

In my experience, the link between my precognition of an event and the actual event is the quality of my own reaction.

Both the moment of foreseeing the event and the moment of experiencing it in its actual time tend to be accompanied by an odd sensation, a kind of mental jolt. It is as though the mind exists simultaneously at two different points in time, but is connected at both points, functioning across time instead of just in the present. Another way to put it is that it is almost as though time has folded at that point and become one experience instead of two. Frequently, my mind is in a relaxed and receptive condition at both points in time.

Over the years, and particularly as a teenager, I had had a number of brief visions of the distant future. Usually, these were fragmentary images seen in almost subliminal flashes that left me with a feeling rather than a complete picture. Quite a number were connected with floods and other natural disasters. I was particularly alerted to climate change as the cause after a teacher pointed out that the glaciers were melting year on year, apparently without realising the significance. These events were often confirmed by news reports.

Some of my premonitions were connected with my family; on one occasion I saw my grandchildren (yet to come). But many were quite unconnected and difficult to place in time, so it was hard to pick out details that might be useful. However, I somehow knew that these belonged to the distant future, and in these the one consistent feature that gave me real cause for concern was the lack of population, both human and animal.

When I have premonitory dreams or visions, I can be fairly certain that they will happen. My short-term precognitions have usually turned out to be true, so I feel I can trust my visions into the more far distant future. The most vivid and long-lasting took place in the early 1980s. On a visit to my friend Peter Harris at his second-hand shop, he suggested that I try some consciously controlled visions of the future, rather than just allowing my visions to come to me. Holding the keys of his cottage, I described his home as it was, and then visualised some changes he had made being reversed. The images picked up speed and became spontaneous as my mind travelled back to the early days of the cottage, about two hundred years before. I made a drawing of it and its location, and some weeks later Peter excitedly told me that he had looked at some old maps in the local library and found that my drawing was entirely accurate for the period.

We then decided that I should try looking into the future, which was surprisingly easy and happened almost instantaneously. I started with the simple expedient of imagining Peter's kitten growing up. Once I had set this in motion I had a feeling of drifting forward, a sort of dissociated floating, which was less unsettling than the falling sensation that accompanied travelling back in time. First I saw Peter suffering a serious but not life-threatening illness; normally, I would not have told him, but felt it safe to do so as I also saw him getting better. About a year later, he had a heart attack, from which he recovered well.

Then, looking further ahead but still in my own lifetime, I saw the cottage empty and knew that many other houses would stand empty and unsold. In the 1980s the area was expanding at a rate that threatened to double the population in ten to fifteen years, but I saw that there would eventually be a drop both in house sales and in the local population.

My forward vision continued as a series of quick glimpses – rather like watching like a fast-forwarding video – until the images came to an automatic stop at a point about two hundred years on. It was a remarkable experience. I saw the same landscape with beautifully cultivated fields; there were no hedgerows or fences, although there were some spinneys of mature trees. I sensed the warm air as being remarkably clean and clear, and there were few or no cars. I somehow knew that there were fewer people around, perhaps a lot fewer. And I could hear no birds, which really bothered me.

It was after this that my other flashes of the future began to fall into place like pieces of a jigsaw. This heightened my interest in exploring the distant future and perhaps finding a possible explanation for this curiously empty world. Deliberate population control would not account for the reduction in animal numbers; environmental factors seemed a much more likely cause. I wanted to know more, and eventually I had the opportunity to find out.

I had almost completed my search for Mary's family when the Easter weekend of 1990 brought with it an odd and unexpected experience. Premonitions and psychic visions can come at any time without warning. On this occasion, Steve was driving us home from Eastbourne, a long journey. As I sat in the passenger seat enjoying the passing landscape, my face towards the setting sun, I relaxed and allowed my mind to drift – which seems to be the ideal state for such experiences.

Running my fingers through my hair, I was aware that the texture had changed: instead of my usually thick, curly hair, the smooth strands under my fingers felt fine, like baby hair, ending in little matted knots. At that point, with considerable surprise, I noticed that my hands were still on my lap. As the altered state continued, it was as though I were two selves at once. I was sufficiently aware of the present to notice

that Steve had put on a cassette tape, and I was simultaneously conscious that my new self belonged to another time,
a future time. Looking down, I saw slender brown legs and
bare feet. I was aware that she/I was an Asian girl of about
two, sitting on the ground daydreaming. Almost instantaneously I accepted her as my future self. I knew she was called
Nadia (with the stress on the 'i'), and that she was a part of
me.

The whole episode probably lasted a minute or two.
Although unexpected, it was not worrying but gentle,
comfortable and reassuring. Perhaps now that the existence
of my past self had been substantiated, I was becoming better
able to accept the reality of a vision of the future. Many may
find this hard to believe, but to me this is an aspect of the
continuity of life. The experience had a different quality from
my memories of Mary. It was as though two-year-old Nadia
was remembering me from her life in the future; perhaps we
were engaged in a kind of telepathy.

After that, it was as though I had opened a door through
which more snatches of my future life began to drift, and
over time I gathered a lot of information about what I knew
was my next life as Nadia, starting around 2040.

More and more images of Nadia's life had come to me –
including her village in the mountains of what I knew to
be eastern Nepal. (Her story is told more fully in *Past Lives,
Future Lives*.) I saw the surrounding landscape in quite a
lot of detail, and Nadia as a young girl looked after by
a woman who could be her grandmother, and then as a
mother herself, working in the fields, with a little boy of
about three playing nearby. These images were usually brief
and fragmentary.

I knew that this future vision was going to be virtually impossible to verify in my own lifetime, but some aspects of the area she lived in could be checked out, since they would probably remain unchanged – including the type of soil, which was red, fine and crumbly, the local geography, the simple food, coinage, vegetation and bird life. As with Mary, I drew some maps, and searched for the area in an atlas.

To gain more information, I decided to try a further experiment in hypnosis. It was five years since my sessions with Jim Alexander; I was not sure whether he would be able or willing to help me to look at the future, but I knew that I could trust him and would feel safe with him in charge. We met for a discussion and he agreed to try hypnotic progression – the term for seeing the future under hypnosis. In October 1993 we embarked on a series of seven experimental sessions. Looking at the future using hypnosis was speculative and needed caution, but with my history of premonition, both spontaneous and sought, I felt that there was some chance of success.

Once again I found myself relaxing in Jim's deep reclining chair, easily slipping into the hypnotic state. Jim's disembodied voice directed me to see time passing until we found the year 2050, and I found myself as Nadia aged eight. In our next few sessions I saw many more details of Nadia's life, including her marriage and the death of a baby. I described the architecture of the region, the red soil, the local clothes, customs, coins, food – in all an amazing amount of detail, which I wrote down as soon as I could after the session.

I described the nearby town that Nadia's family visited about once a month, frequently on the occasion of a religious festival. In the town there was a temple with a wide-angled

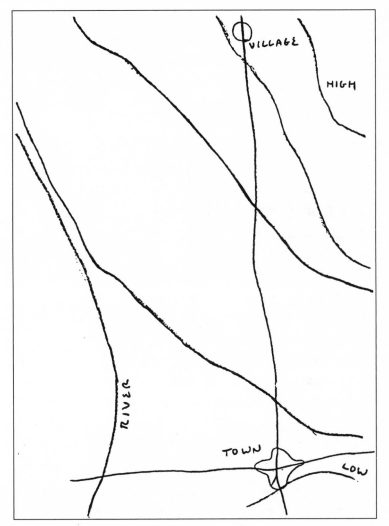

My first sketch of the area near Nadia's village

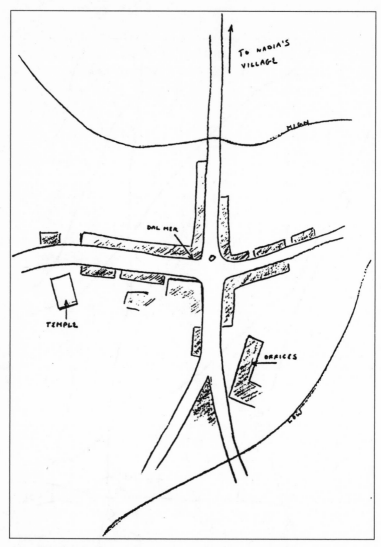

A sketch map of the town near Nadia's village, showing positions of various buildings of importance

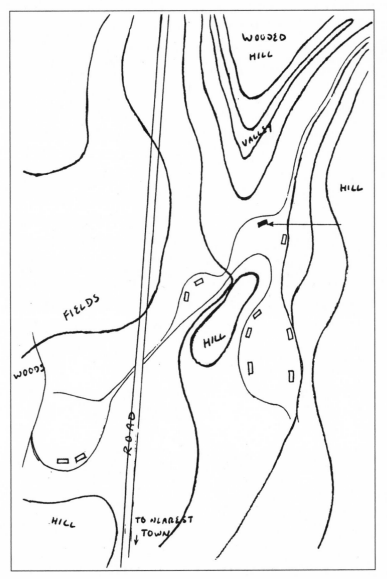

A more detailed sketch map of the area surrounding Nadia's home

pitched roof and decoration along the front edge, carved in stone and consisting of many identical three-part pieces, a little like fleurs-de-lys, with spherical tops. Asked what I bought at the shops, I said that most of them sold things we didn't need (or probably could not afford). The goods on sale were mainly locally made, and were usually bought by 'the people who pass through'. This suggested tourists, but I had a strong feeling that much was sold to the increasing number of American development workers who were billeted in the new government buildings in the town centre.

It seemed that there was a hydroelectric plant being developed with foreign help, and I had the feeling that other projects were under way further afield. When Jim asked whether I knew what was in the news, I was aware that Central Africa was going through turbulent times, and the other main subject of conversation was China, which concerned me more. The news was something to do with

Sketch of the decorated temple roof

power and governments, but there was a background fear that whatever was going on threatened our stability. Afterwards I wondered about this. China took over Tibet in the 1950s; could China be posing a threat to Nepal in the 2060s?

Because it was so easy to see things under hypnosis I sometimes had qualms that not everything might be real or accurate, yet at the same time I was quite certain that Nadia was my future self. What I had not expected was my tremendous sense of relief. Perhaps I had been afraid that what I knew would be a simple life might also be full of hardship, but this was not the case. I was left with a feeling of a terrific zest for life and enjoyment of every facet of living. Although it was a fairly basic existence, there was no sense of lack – even though my education and opportunities would be limited in this life. There was a richness and warmth in the companionship of family and friends that remained in my consciousness, brightening the present.

Tiny flashes of Nadia's life were coming to me quite often without hypnosis. There was one particular scene that recurred quite often, when I found myself focusing on a few moments of one particular day. I was standing at home looking out of the window, doing nothing, just looking and somehow waiting. I was alone apart from the first child, asleep in her cot. What seemed significant about this scene was Nadia's frame of mind. It was a calm, meditative, almost resigned feeling. It was also the kind of state that I recognised as conducive to psychic experiences. Perhaps that was why I kept touching into this time frame, experiencing this tiny moment across the years.

However, when Jim asked me to look ahead to Nadia at forty, it was a shock to find nothing there. For a brief spell I felt as if I were teetering on the edge of a precipice, and then I was drawn back to the present. For a while afterwards I was quite disturbed by this – perhaps it had revived my fears of dying young like Mary. However, I had had forewarnings of difficult times in the past and managed to carry on my daily life. This helped me to acquire a kind of emotional detachment regarding precognition, and soon I was able to apply this to my future as Nadia.

Once my hypnosis sessions were over, I did a good deal of research into present-day Nepal, and the details tallied with my visions – such as the red soil, the architecture, plants, wildlife and some of the customs. I even found, on a detailed map, the hill where I believe Nadia will live.

Although Nadia's life may be short – which would be in keeping with that of Nepalese women today – it will be a relaxed and peaceful one. In my present life I tend to be driven; any idle moments are quickly filled. But Nadia's life, which may be influenced by both Buddhism and Hinduism, has a laid-back, happy quality. I look forward to it almost as a holiday!

★　★　★

There was one session when Jim decided to approach our experiment a little differently. He asked me to imagine going down some stairs at the bottom of which I would see an infinitely long corridor lined with many doors. Behind each door was a different memory stored in the subconscious. I began to move forward past several doors – a red door, then a blue one, moving on until I came to a golden-yellow door with light spilling out around the edges.

Opening it, I first saw just brilliant light, then a tree beneath which sat an old man, his head bowed in contemplation. As I began to recognise where I was, the tree became pure light. I knew that I was in a between-lives state. The man was an old friend; his name was Ram. Without speaking or gesturing, he welcomed me.

As I described this to Jim, my voice slowed down. 'I know this place . . . It's all right . . . Nothing matters now.'

'Have you been here before?' Jim asked.

'Many times . . . Always.'

Bathed in the light and completely at peace, I allowed joy to encompass me. This, I told Jim, was a healing place between lives. (Afterwards I realised that I had been experiencing the first moments after Nadia's death.) I would have liked to stay there much longer, but he moved me on to another door, asking me to find a sad memory. And there was Nadia at about twenty-one, cradling the lifeless form of her tiny daughter. Tears rolled down my cheeks as Nadia and I wept together.

But this time, there was something different about the sense of loss, which resulted from my visit to the between-lives state. Remembering that incredible radiant light and the all-enveloping calm, I understood fully that all experience is transitory.

During my very last hypnosis session, Jim asked me to look at a period beyond the end of Nadia's life. This was distressing. The time was somewhere around 2150 and I was in mainland Europe, possibly Poland. I was cradling my husband's head and comforting him as he died, aged only about fifty. There was evidence of poverty and hardship and a sense of stress and resignation that went beyond the grief of the moment; it was clear that life was hard. The only positive feelings were the will to survive and my love for my husband, who I felt was the same person as Steve. This is probably the lowest moment in our future history; the lives to come after it were much more positive.

Next, when Jim asked me again to explore the corridor with its infinity of doors, I was drawn to one made of textured wood and opened it to find myself touching the fissured bark of a huge tree. My first comment was about the thickness and sponginess of the bark. I was a dumpy single woman; I gave my age as 'the wrong side of thirty' and my name, tentatively as always, as Janice Thorpe. The date was 16 June 2228. I wasn't really interested in answering Jim's questions – I had work to do. My job was to take a core sample of this giant tree, which would be passed on for study for its possible medical or other uses.

I was doing fieldwork for Unichem in South America, which I enjoyed; back home in Jersey, USA, I did lab work. I had quite a lot to say about my work and, interestingly, about the area where I lived. Although population decline was not obvious, there were a number of buildings standing empty.

We spoke about pollution. The air was clean – Janice remarked that 'plants are pretty good at cleaning the air if you let them get on with it. The air's not a big problem – it's mostly in water and in the food chain.' The sea, she said, was badly polluted and could not be used as a source of food. Nobody was allowed to pump pollutants into the sea any more, but over the years there had been a general toxic build-up that had spread through all the oceans, as water-soluble chemicals had been carried out from the land and would take a long time to break down.

During this conversation Jim asked whether I knew what was the most important scientific discovery or invention over the last hundred years. All that came to my mind was a beam of light used for diagnosis in hospitals and laboratory analysis, apparently an extension of laser technology. It seemed to work by taking measurements of the interruptions to light as the beam passed through living tissues, showing up abnormalities due to frequency changes. The beam was also used on core samples from plants, as the first stage of analysis.

Three years after this session, and just too late to include it in *Past Lives, Future Lives*, I read the following item in the *Daily Telegraph* for Wednesday, 21 February 1996:

A laser microscope that can study the activity and behaviour of living cells, down to the activity of tens of individual molecules in volumes as small as one tenth of a millionth of a millionth of a sugar cube, has been developed by Prof. Watt Webb's team at Cornell University. These advanced microscopes can reveal fundamental biological processes in living cells – metabolism, wound healing, cancer cell behaviour, and nerve cell communication, opening up a whole new world for biologists.

This was clearly what I had described as Janice. Any form of verification is useful in precognition, and to have the development of this prototype invention published three years after I had described a more advanced model under hypnosis was extremely reassuring.

The next life chronologically was that of another American, Sheryl Vaughn; we returned to her more than once. At our first encounter she was a slight, blonde fifteen-year-old living in California in the year 2285. It seemed to be a time full of hope and enthusiasm.

We were in a classroom, in a mixed-age study group discussing ideas about time and physics, and how all subjects were interlinked. 'It's about how to understand how time affects us, how we use time to understand other ideas,' I told Jim. My first answers came with many pauses – I wanted to hear what the teacher was saying. There were enthusiastic responses from my fellow students; it seemed we were there because we wanted to gain from the experience of learning rather than because we had to be there. As well as being traditionally taught by a teacher, we learned by listening to recordings – the best way to learn, according to Sheryl. We also used computers, linked to small networks.

Visiting Sheryl at the age of twenty-five, I told Jim that some buildings stood empty, confirming the idea of a reduction in population. But what was particularly striking was a sense of safety and security. I had the feeling that I could happily leave my house with the front door unlocked.

I told Jim that I worked from home using a console linked to agency computers. I described my home and my workstation in detail, and explained to Jim that my job was to do with the living sciences, with plants and animals and the interdependent relationships between living things. I talked at some length about my work, which was to collect information on plant strains resistant to pests and diseases, and the best areas to grow them in. The aim was to increase production without using chemicals – soils were still heavily damaged by excessive chemical use in the past, which had also affected water supplies. We used solar energy and other renewable sources rather than burning coal or oil; there were still some problems with oil pollution, and we used bacteria to consume the oil.

I told Jim there had been two periods of high pollution, one at the beginning of the Industrial Revolution, and the later era (coinciding with our present times) when chemical pollution was the main problem. During this phase, the birds had been the first to suffer, although they still survived in some areas. Marine animals were also suffering from a heavily polluted environment, but they were still holding out, including a few species of whale. All living creatures, including people, had suffered some damage from the cocktail of chemicals; the main effect seemed to be infertility, and there had been a considerable drop in the human population. There had also been difficulties with the atmosphere, but these were relatively easy to correct in time.

One of my assumptions before these sessions was that a major cause of environmental problems would be an increase in sunlight, due to damage to the ozone layer. But Sheryl pretty well dismissed this idea. It could be that the problem will be solved by the reduction in pollution, including traffic pollution, and assisted by the reduction in human numbers.

Although it was not touched on during these sessions, I had been aware of the problems of global warming since 1964 (long before it was recognised) when I had several dreams about future flooding and seemed to be the only person worried about melting glaciers. When we bought our home in 1975 flood risk was not a usual consideration, but it was my first thought.

It is significant that both my Janice and Sheryl personalities had an interest in ecological science and worked in botanical research. This suggests both a continuity and a development of interests and skills, which supports the theory that people can bring into a new life skills already learned in a previous one. One of my own main areas of interest has been human biology, but I can easily envisage developing an interest in plants.

Of course it is impossible to prove the reality of a future life. I realised that there were only two ways to find out whether precognition of the distant future had a chance of being right. One was to look back at earlier insights for their accuracy; this was not a problem. The other was to look at present trends to see whether any of them might already be leading us towards the envisaged future. At the time I was not aware of the wealth of information available about changes to the environment, and consequently to our health and fertility, resulting from chemical pollution. Since 1993, when I looked into this possible future, more and more information has come to light about the effects of chemical pollution on our environment and our health. The use of fermented fuel or biofuels for vehicles, which are clean and renewable, unlike oil-based products, is already being developed.

The two accounts included consistencies in the descriptions of environmental and population changes. Today we are much more aware of the rapidly increasing problems with male fertility, which is apparently due to male foetuses being exposed to female-hormone-mimicking chemicals that damage fertility before birth. Some surveys suggest that one in five couples now experience fertility problems. Present trends could well explain the reduction in population in the future.

Although we have created a difficult situation for ourselves on this planet, the future I saw was full of hope. It may not be a perfect existence, but the air will be clean and the crops healthy. There will be fewer people (rather than the unprecedented overpopulation currently predicted by many scientists) and they will be combining a sensible control of the environment with a greater understanding of their responsibility for the wellbeing of the whole. Although I saw life only in the West, Sheryl's work in America seemed to involve international cooperation, at least in the world of ecology and food production, and there was little sense of national borders. Could it be that we will be expending our intelligence and resources on environmental care rather than on warfare and enmity? Perhaps the global movement of people already occurring could lead to this cooperation.

Each time Jim progressed me to the distant future, he asked whether there was violence or danger in the society. Each time, I answered that there was not, in a tone expressing surprise at being asked such a question. A reduction in crime and violence could be one beneficial result of reduced population; overcrowding and poverty would be eradicated and there would be employment for everyone. And a lower birthrate would mean that children are really wanted and valued.

Past Lives, Future Lives was published in 1996. I included in it details of my other previous lives, my experiment in future hypnosis, my environmental concerns and research related to it and to premonitory experiences dating back to my childhood. I had written much of it many years earlier and it required a great deal of editorial assistance to link the various items of subject matter. In part it resulted from the energy generated from resolving my past as Mary: I was still running on adrenalin and found that further writing and researching helped to calm me down. It was also a chance to put down everything I had not felt able to include in *Yesterday's Children*, particularly the memory of dying as Mary, the between-lives experiences and various psychic episodes which I had previously felt somewhat embarrassed by and reluctant to discuss.

CHAPTER 15

Life Between Lives

When I underwent hypnosis to help with my past-life research, the times between lives was not explored at all. Jim suggested that I see these periods as dark, and my subconscious followed his suggestions – apart from the episode following Nadia's death (described in Chapter 14). However, I knew inside myself that these periods were not dark, but full of light.

Along with my memories of Mary Sutton's life, I had always had a memory not only of her dying, but of a continued existence after her death. For a long time I felt nervous about sharing this with anyone; it seemed so far from most people's experience, and I had no way of proving that it had been real.

As Mary, I was alone when I was dying, the loneliness adding to my burden of grief at leaving my children behind. At the moment of death, I knew that I had died. I knew that I was leaving the body, not just drifting out of it but suddenly thrust out, rather like a buoy cut loose from its moorings. After this swift upward rush, I was aware of settling some ten feet above the body and slightly to one side of it. Although I was actually above the ceiling, I could see the room clearly.

I remained there for some time, long enough to see a man come to the bedside. How much time had passed it is hard to say, as my sense of time in this state was very vague, and certainly irrelevant.

What happened from this point on was no less clear. I was still looking back at my now vacant body when I seemed to be drawn from behind – almost sucked – into a long, narrow tube, like a fold in space, a dark vortex that wrapped round me and drew me into another dimension. Through it I travelled backwards, feeling somehow folded as though in a loose foetal position. Slowly the hospital room drifted away from me, growing smaller and smaller until finally it faded completely.

Now, intensely bright beams of light began to emerge on either side of me, like the shafts of a rainbow, though much, much brighter. To describe them as light seems somehow insufficient: the rainbow colours were much more vibrant than normal light, just as a real rainbow is much more vibrant than one drawn in crayons. The shafts of light passed by me at different angles, then spread out as though radiating from a central focus.

I don't remember the actual moment when I emerged into a different place, but I know that I did emerge into somewhere very gentle and peaceful, far beyond any normal understanding of the words. This part is not clear in my memory, although it seems to be the stage remembered most clearly by people who have had near-death experiences (NDEs). This is when they have usually found themselves meeting other people and/or going through a review of their lives. It seems possible, too, that it is from this stage that people usually return, in dreams or in spirit form, if they need to communicate with those they have left behind.

Some of their descriptions include beautiful gardens and vivid rainbows.

My brother Michael, from whom I was estranged, died in the summer of 1986 when my daughter Heather was just three. As we had been unable to visit Michael or his family for a long time, Heather hardly knew him. Then, within two weeks of his death, Heather told me that she had had a strange dream that was 'not a dream', during which my 'magic brother' had visited her. I asked her why he was magic and she explained that he had been able to 'magic' himself into her room, and had shown her a 'rainbow garden'. As well as a three-year-old could, she told me about a garden that was not here but somewhere else, and that it was special; she knew that what had happened was different from everyday life and ordinary dreams. She was a little confused and hesitant about talking about it, so I didn't press her to tell me more at the time.

I did tell my mother about the incident, and, when we visited her a week later, Heather was happy to tell her grandmother about my magic brother and the rainbow garden. On the day of Michael's death – which of course had been very distressing for her – my mother had been away on a camping holiday, where she had seen a spectacular rainbow.

Heather's story not only gave comfort to my mother, but also gave me courage. It was actually one of the catalysts that set me off on my search for my past-life children, because it helped me to accept the validity of my own experiences. It was also healing for my relationship with Michael. He had been a padre in the RAF and before that an Anglican vicar, and in life his views differed radically from mine. Yet it was Michael who brought us this vision – a vision of heaven, but one from which it is possible to return. For me this was compensation enough for the many things we had not been able to agree upon. It was as though he had found a way to tell me we were *both* right.

People who have NDEs are likely to remember the stage of arrival clearly because it is the one from which they return to life more or less directly. All I can remember of this time is that for a while there was a lot going on, some of which was perhaps to do with other people and some to my adjustment to my new state of being. What remains most clearly with me is the stage that followed: it is still crystal clear.

I found myself floating inside something like a soap bubble. Above, below and all around me were other bubbles that I knew to be people. I was bodiless, and this didn't matter at all, since there was no need for a body. The other bubbles seemed to have the peaceful energies of other people, also without bodies yet seemingly complete, and I felt a total, peaceful empathy with them.

The sensation was of being almost like a single cell within a whole constellation of cells, yet also of being far too much of an individual entity to be contained in one small unit. I was still aware of being myself, an individual soul. Every bubble glowed brightly with an energy that I took to be the basic life force that is ourselves, and they pulsated at rhythms that varied from a slow heartbeat to a steady vibration.

There was a great deal of background light all around, as though the whole life energy was expressed as light. It was difficult to see beyond it – it seemed to be reflected a little like the reflection of headlights in fog. Some of it took the form of strands like energy bands, mainly white through to blue in colour. The overall feeling was of white light energy.

Enveloping everything was a feeling of calm in which nothing seemed to matter or hurt or cause anxiety. Here the existence I had left behind seemed no more than a vague memory. Perhaps it simply became less important as time passed – though the notion of time itself had almost no meaning. There was no demarcation between day and night, just constant, peaceful light. Yet there was no sense of boredom – which, I find, is difficult for people to understand. This state of being is so utterly different from physical life that it is hard to put into words, but without bodies there is no need for activities and diversions. It is enough just to be. Yet, although apparently inactive, we seemed to end up as more than we were when we started.

The bubble energies that were other people seemed to feel close all around me – yet this was nothing like being in a crowd of bodies. I had the sensation of being surrounded and enfolded by what I can only describe as love. There was a wonderful sense of being incorporated with some much larger dimension of existence.

Although I never had any doubt about the reality of this memory, I hesitated for a long time to speak of it to anyone. However, I gained confidence as I began to read about NDEs described by growing numbers of people who have returned to life after being pronounced clinically dead for several minutes. The more I found out, the more I recognised the similarities to my own memories of dying as Mary.

My memories of earlier deaths associated with other past lives are less distinct. With the Japanese life that ended in drowning, the tunnel was more like a vortex. As the water seemed to move aside, there appeared to be an anticlockwise rotational movement of the tunnel, not unlike water going down a plughole, except that it was moving upwards. On this occasion, I travelled facing forward and at the end of the tunnel I saw white light, sparkling with flashes of colour. In addition there seemed to be someone there to meet me at the end of the tunnel, but I remember no more than that.

Most people experiencing NDEs describe an out-of-body experience that is instantaneous with the cessation of signs of life. It is common to see one's physical body below one, while the spiritual self that contains self-awareness is positioned above and often a little to one side of the body. Several people have been able to give accurate accounts of what was going on around them while they were clinically dead, and some have even described activities going on in the next room. This adds considerable weight to the idea that, at death, the consciousness or spirit leaves the physical body but can still observe its surroundings. At this stage there is usually a feeling of retaining an echo of one's physical shape.

Next, most people describe travelling down a tunnel, usually forwards, looking towards a bright, white light at the end. A number – often children – have described seeing rainbow-coloured light. Some people have described rolling into a ball when passing through the tunnel – reminding me of my folded-up foetal position while in transit. The most important part of the experience, and the one most consistently referred to, is a feeling of absolute peace and wellbeing as one reaches the light.

Sometimes a sense of light or peace occurs shortly before dying, and some people on the point of death have suddenly become aware of a lost relative standing nearby, waiting for them. One of my patients told me how she sat with her mother as she was dying. It was a dull, overcast day and her mother, who was terminally ill, had been listless and unresponsive for some time. Quite suddenly she looked past the daughter into a shadowy corner of the room and said, 'How beautiful! The sun is shining!' She died shortly afterwards, and her sense of upliftment and joy during her last moments helped her daughter to accept her death in a totally unlooked-for way.

After death, many people continue to see spiritual energies in human form, describing them as people dressed in white and glowing with light. When I was surrounded by the bubble energies, I was aware that they were people, and, although they were nonphysical, they seemed to emanate friendliness.

It was not until I read *Transformed by the Light* by Dr Melvin Morse and Paul Perry (Piatkus, 1993) that I came across a description similar to my own experience of energy bubbles. In this serious study of NDEs, the case study of 'Patient 44' recounts that she remembered having no body and being contained within 'some kind of essence' similar to the gelatine capsule used to contain medicines. The book also includes descriptions by others of being 'a ball of light'. For me this was a revelation. It was the first time I had read an account that so completely tallied with my own memories of the between-lives state, and it was extremely reassuring.

In an earlier study of NDEs, *Life After Life* (Mockingbird Books, 1975) Dr Raymond Moody found that, of the details given by his interviewees, nine came up most frequently, and of these most people mentioned a few. They are: a sense of being dead; feelings of peace and painlessness; an out-of-body experience; travelling down a tunnel; seeing people of light; being greeted by a particular being of light; undergoing a life review; a reluctance to return; and a personality trans-formation after returning to life.

My own memory of between lives incorporates the first five elements. My memory was of course a long-term one, recalled from the time before my birth into this life, and is therefore different from NDEs, which are usually brief and vivid. In my case I have no clear picture of meetings with other people or of the life review, during which people look back over their lives in order to evaluate their actions.

The life review usually occurs after one first arrives in the other plane after death. Some people report that they have experienced the events of their lives from the perspective of others, so that they have felt the pain that they themselves have inflicted. In taking the role of the victims of their own misdeeds they understand the hurt their actions may have caused.

A vivid account of this kind of life review is given in *Saved by the Light* by Dannion Brinkley, who has survived two NDEs. He makes it clear that judging oneself is not something to be thought of lightly, because experiencing the results of our own actions can be unimaginably punishing. While I have no memory of the life review itself, I seem to have retained some consciousness of it, in that I have been left with a very strong feeling that we are not judged by others or by some divine authority: we judge ourselves. This means that only we can take responsibility for our actions and change ourselves. And, ultimately, we have to forgive ourselves.

In the summer of 1994 I was invited to take part in a confer-ence on reincarnation and rebirth in Oslo, organised by the Norwegian psychologist and author Dr Rune Amundsen. I had never spoken in public before, so the experience was initially rather daunting, but it was well worth it.

One of the guest speakers was Dannion Brinkley. After struggling with words to describe the totally enveloping sense of peace and lack of negative emotions, the feeling of being a part of a larger energy and not isolated, and the light and vibrancy of the between-lives period, I was uplifted by Dannion's reassurance when we spoke afterwards. It was a great relief that someone with such a vivid memory of his own NDEs was able to identify with my memory of the between-lives phase. It was also reassuring to speak with other people who shared similar memories, such as the suddenness of moving out of the body. Until that time I had felt very alone with my experiences.

Fortunately, I had always had access to some relevant reference works. One of the best known is the *Bardo Thodol*, known as *The Tibetan Book of the Dead*. This ancient text is designed to be read aloud to the dying and the newly dead to guide them through the afterlife, so that they can reach Nirvana, the state of absolute blessedness in which one is liberated from the cycle of reincarnation. The description of the first state arrived at is very similar to modern NDE accounts, including brilliant light and feelings of extreme peace. Also mentioned are out-of-body experiences and a halo of rainbow light, also common in NDEs.

But there was one state, described quite a long way into the text, that I instantly recognised because it was so similar to my main memory of the between-lives state. This is called the 'Central Realm of the Densely Packed', where one merges into the halo of rainbow light in which one obtains Buddha-hood. It reminded me very much of my feelings of being bathed in light and surrounded on all sides by an apparently infinite number of other light-emitting energies, closely packed together and resonating with each other. There does seem to be an anomaly here, since this is the state leading to Nirvana from which one need not return, yet I experienced it and still felt the need to return.

The sense of the energy between lives as all-inclusive, that as single entities we are not alone but a part of something greater, is not necessarily confined to the between-lives states. It has been experienced by mystics of all religions, and also by people going about their ordinary lives, as I did when I was in my teens – an experience that has left me with the certainty of the connectedness of all life.

If my visions of the future are reliable, one effect of the reduction in population could be that we will not have to return so rapidly from the realm of light to re-enter a physical body, and a more natural rhythm will be restored to the ebb and flow of these two life states. It is possible that staying longer in the between-lives state could mean a greater chance of returning with some of the feelings of love and connectedness experienced in that state, making a positive contribution to the next physical life and those with whom we interact.

Whatever we experience and learn in that restful between-lives state, I am convinced that our role on this planet is intended as one of action and interaction. When we take on physical bodies, the spiritual lesson is about learning to live in harmony with each other and with our environment. Living within a body gives us the opportunity to face the demands of life, and to grow and learn. All we can do as individuals is to try to understand our role in events and to try to take the right action at the right time. Our shared responsibility must be to humanity in general.

CHAPTER 16

Conclusion

The search for my past lives has been a long, fascinating and at times painful journey. It has helped me to resolve inner conflicts, stemming both from this life and past ones. It has enabled me to understand myself better, and also others close to me, especially my father. It has forced me to face my fears. In some ways the experience of researching past lives has been more important than finding the answers. Even when it has not been possible to resolve everything completely, I have still benefited from a learning process. Most importantly, my quest has released me from guilt and made me aware of the need for self-forgiveness.

It has also brought me opportunities for growth and expansion. The success of *Yesterday's Children* enabled me to travel and to meet experts in the field of reincarnation, and faced me with challenges such as having to speak in public. And one benefit of the publicity I have received, and the fact that I have been able to prove the reality of my life as Mary Sutton, is that others with past-life memories may be reassured that their experiences are quite normal.

Even so, researching past lives is not something I would recommend to everyone. However, if you feel this is something you need to do, I hope, by sharing all the pitfalls, to help make your own journey easier to cope with.

The question of why we are here has preoccupied human-kind for centuries, and today – despite the disorder in the world, or perhaps because of it – many people are on a spiritual path. The belief in reincarnation is gaining credibility, some of it owing to a growing body of convincing research, some of it owing to a greater spiritual openness.

It is often said that we are all on a spiritual journey; this is supported by the life review described in the previous chapter, which has been frequently reported by people returning from near-death experiences. This review, which takes place very soon after death, obliges us to look back and see how we treated others during the most recent life, and is a form both of self-appraisal and self-punishment, compelling us to feel exactly the way we have made others feel. It is simple and direct, with no ambiguity; we know instantly if we have caused pain or engendered love. It is much more likely to arouse a sense of responsibility for one's actions than judgement by some authority. And in itself it suggests that there is an intention to learn and to improve, to use the next life as an opportunity for spiritual growth.

★   ★   ★

Although there are many theories about the mechanisms of reincarnation, my experiences have led me to draw my own conclusions. Evidence, particularly in the form of personal experience, is more important to me than any beliefs or theories, but there is one thing I am quite certain of: that we have all lived before and will all live again. Over the course of history we have all been many people in a variety of situations and localities. So who are we? We are timeless, free spiritual beings who repeatedly try out physicality, with all its pitfalls, in order to gain understanding. The person you are now is a mixture from three main sources. We are formed first by what we inherit from our parents, and, second, by our environment and upbringing. We also have a core personality that is carried from life to life, that evolves with us.

None of my past-life memories has put me in a prominent position, or even in particularly dramatic times. Statistically speaking, this would seem reasonable, since the majority of people live unremarkable lives and you can expect your own past lives to be equally ordinary. I missed the French Revolution by a few years and was a very young child during the Second World War. Several of my lives have been very short. The most prestigious was in Japan, the rest I spent often in poverty, and twice I was a very withdrawn little boy.

Certain themes recur, including more than one instance of a violent father or husband, and an ongoing sense of responsibility for failure and guilt for dying too soon. Above all, I am very aware of having been the same person throughout these lives; for me, the consistent feature is the development of the self through a series of changing circumstances. Change is essential for growth and each life has its particular set of challenges. Reincarnation is rather like going through a series of jobs in different cities; one gains experience through meeting different demands. Over the course of one life we slowly change and grow; over the course of many lives this process may continue. The spirit remains the same, released at death to rest between lives in another dimension.

Over the millennia, since life first emerged on our planet,

all living beings have evolved. Creatures change, possibly in response to environmental pressures, possibly at random – when only the successful changes survive. Life is a continuous, growing, developing process. As nature learns what works and what does not, the changes may become less marked, but there are still changes, refining the successes already achieved.

In reincarnation a similar evolution may also occur. As we inhabit a variety of bodies we may be given the chance to learn different things, and go through a variety of experiences that require new responses. Some part of this learning process can be carried over from life to life, and thus we have the chance to evolve emotionally and spiritually.

It is this opportunity to evolve as spiritual beings that makes sense of our short lives. The process derives meaning from the changes that we undergo and what we can do through understanding these changes. What we can take with us from life to life is more than just a mix of memories; what is important is what we have learned from those lives.

It goes further. The whole of life on this planet has to function as a unit. We derive life from other living things, plants and animals, and need these to be healthy and thrive for our own continued existence. Civilisation has to mean that we work with the systems of nature to develop what we need and find useful, and we have at last begun to realise that where we destroy in order to fulfil our needs we also have to rebuild.

In a sense, life on this planet functions as one; everything is interconnected. Scientific discoveries and inventions often occur simultaneously at several places in the world. This is partly because the information available reaches a point at which a particular change or development becomes possible. But I also believe that events occur simultaneously because, at a deeply subconscious level, we function as a single unit, a collective mind.

Carl Jung, the pioneer psychoanalyst, described the collective unconscious, which may be reached through emotional responses, and is outside of time. It is unchanging, singular and nonpersonal. The collective unconscious might be described as the whole of nature, to which we are all connected. It may be how we access visions of future events, because where time is irrelevant there is no before or after. It is in a way where we all exist together, regardless of where or who we are.

One reason why research into reincarnation has recently become more successful is that information in the form of records is more widely available. People today share their interests more openly and widely, and have reached a stage of tolerance towards attitudes different from their own. But I believe there is another reason. Our group consciousness, albeit unconsciously, shares information. If a few people are working on an idea, any idea, it seeps through to other people because we are connected.

We are usually aware of only a tiny fraction of our own existence. Accepting that we have lived before is only half the story: there is also the time between lives, the time when we reconnect. This may be where we really exist, where we remember everything and assess what we have learned as we become immersed in the entire energy of life. The impression I have retained from my memories of the between-lives state is that sooner or later the spiritual self feels an urge to return, a kind of wanting to be. It seems likely that this need to re-experience life in a physical form is prompted by the need to do or learn something in order to feel complete and fulfilled. So what makes us choose to come back at particular times and under particular circumstances?

My own experience and gut feelings do not always correspond with some of the traditional teachings or current New Age thinking. For example, I do not believe that we choose our parents or our next birthplace in any conscious sense. Nor do I feel that we are reborn into difficult circumstances as a punishment for past misdeeds. After all, a difficult life provides greater challenges than a comfortable one and can be seen as providing an opportunity for learning and self-development. Life is not easy for most people, much of the time. It is probably not meant to be easy; we learn more about ourselves and each other by facing up to challenges.

In fact, I feel that the hardship or otherwise of the lives we choose is almost incidental; disabilities are neither inflicted nor chosen but purely the result of genetic accidents. Factors such as race and social circumstances exist in the physical state; between lives they are totally irrelevant. It seems that our return from that state is much more like being drawn towards certain circumstances and people by subconscious instinct – just as we are instinctively drawn to friendships – rather than by rational calculation.

The mind is more closely linked to the spirit than is the body, but while the ability to make good use of one's intelligence may depend on the personality, intelligence itself is likely to be inherited. What seems most consistently to continue from one life to the next is the personality, which is the expression of the spirit, and which needs to acquire new experiences in order to learn and grow.

We have three parts to us that should, ideally, be equal and balanced. The body needs work, exercise and proper nutrition to maintain physical health. The mind needs challenges and communication. The soul is partly about timelessness and being connected to others but is also about our responsibilities, how we make others feel and how we care.

Things that are important to the soul are unlikely to be the things that the body might appreciate as good or bad. A simple, ordinary life, even with the problems that many people have to cope with, such as disability, can be good and rewarding as long as one's family and friends are open, loving and caring. In choosing a new life, it is the soul that makes the choice, and the soul is not materialistic. I believe that it is the rewards that are experienced on our return to the between-lives state, as much as the joy of living, that make life worth the effort.

If we choose a particular emphasis in a particular life, it may be in order to balance aspects of the personality that are slightly out of kilter. In my current life, for instance, I have found myself – like many women today – in circumstances that have ultimately led me to give up the role of 'victim', in which early childhood placed me, in order to become more myself. Someone else might need to learn to become less aggressive or arrogant. Or our needs may be to do with using our lives creatively, to cultivate our gifts and talents.

I believe that an important reason for coming back is to heal relationships, both with others and ourselves. It seems that we are often drawn to share several lives with particular people. (This accounts for the feeling people often have of 'knowing' someone they have never met before.) They may be loved ones – I have known my husband in past lives, and know that we will be together again in the future. Often, they are people with whom we need to resolve difficulties. If we have a problem with someone, this may be the opportunity to heal an emotional situation we have carried with us through several past lives.

My own experience suggests that many of us feel a need for forgiveness, particularly self-forgiveness. This may be an important factor in drawing us to particular life circumstances. The burden of carrying negative emotions, either through one life or from one life to the next, is destructive both to ourselves and to others. The need to let go of or come to terms with them may be a strong element in our next choice of life.

I have been contacted by several young men who have past-life memories as soldiers in the Vietnam War. Significantly, they describe a sense of guilt that was probably beyond their actual culpability. There is a belief that they should have done more – to save friends, to prevent atrocities, to help others. Sometimes people take on more guilt than they deserve; in such cases, good hypnotherapy can help to put the past into perspective, but any form of healing after such an ordeal can take time and needs to be undertaken with a great deal of care.

Our sense of guilt is not always a true gauge of our responsibility, and may be disproportionate. By contrast, however, there are also some cases where self-forgiveness has to come out of accepting the true reality, however terrible, rather than deflecting blame on circumstances. Unfortunately, we live in a culture of blame – and blame, of ourselves, of others, or of our past lives, is not conducive to healing relationships.

When I renewed my relationship with my father I had

many long discussions with him, to the point where I came to understand how his pain had contributed to what he described as his failure as a parent. Working with him helped me to develop a useful approach to other problems as well as repairing the relationship. Resolution started from the point when I realised that there was greater healing possible through helping him than could ever be achieved by releasing my anger. The time bomb was defused, not exploded. By working through the past with him and giving up blame it became easier to apply the same process and defuse negative and self-destructive emotions caused by other situations.

Although I felt driven to undertake my research, I don't believe that everyone would necessarily benefit from learning about their past lives – indeed, I believe that we are meant to forget them and move on. It is not necessary to have recall of past lives to understand and accept their reality, or to have a sense of the continuity of the soul. Nor is it essential to have a near-death experience to appreciate that life continues after we leave the body or to trust in the promise of tremendous peace and happiness in that other existence. We do not have to have visions of the future in order to have hope for the future of our species. Those who believe that we live only once may not care what the world will be like in two hundred years' time. But, if we are aware that we live many lifetimes, the picture changes radically. Our future selves will continue to live with the consequences of how we act now.

It may be that our present problems have their roots in previous lives, but looking to past lives for the answers may not be the solution. It is in the present that we need to change and grow, to recognise and meet challenges and difficulties. We cannot go back to a past life, even if we can remember it.

In all probability we may be reunited with a past love, dear friends and family members in many of these lives, and also between lives. But looking backwards instead of forwards may not be helpful. In each life we change a little, we grow a little; we cannot be the people we once were. The only way forward is to acknowledge the truth of our feelings, and let go of the past. Then we may realise that all we hope for is ahead of us.

If we could stand back from ourselves and question the motivation behind certain responses and actions, we might realise that many of our attitudes or instinctive reactions are obsolete. To be the best we can be it may be necessary to question our actions, to try to resolve the past and learn to change. Even if we can change only one small aspect of ourselves at a time, it is worth the effort.

Some of our emotional responses are liable to be inherited or learned. Many emotions are linked to physical existence and have no place in the core, spiritual self. Fear, anger, hate and envy are all to do with physical survival and may be unavoidable in hostile conditions. But the spirit that is the core being within each of us does not need them. Our spirit does not need to fight to survive.

We may find that the core, our true personality, surfaces when we are able to act outside the restrictions of our upbringing and environment, or in the subtle ways in which we respond to the needs of others. It may be the part of us that surfaces in a crisis, when we reach deeper inside ourselves before we act. I think that we can all be aware of the real person inside if we give ourselves a chance to stop fighting life and open up to possibilities. The real self is likely to be the inner voice that gives us love and hope.

I feel that the reason we are all here, the purpose of each individual, may be something quite small. We do not have to do anything world-changing, but in small ways we can help to change humanity as a species, so that together we move slowly towards real civilisation. Because we are all connected, the small ways in which we can change can help to make the whole organism of life function a bit better. And all that we can take with us into the next life is our intent.

Although I was extraordinarily lucky to be able to find the children from my Irish life, and at least to begin to resolve some of the issues that appear to be related to many pasts, the answer I needed all along was to accept and understand that the past has gone. What we are given is the present and the future. What is precious is the here and now, who we are now and the people around us now.

APPENDIX

The Difficulties of Researching Past Lives

I have always liked to back up my psychic experiences with solid evidence. My search for Mary Sutton's family was a long piece of detective work, and it was thrilling when at last I obtained objective evidence of what I had always known. Researching my Japanese life probably went as far as it could under difficult circumstances. I have also attempted to trace two other previous lives. It is a slow, painstaking process. In the first instance I had a degree of success, but the second illustrates all the difficulties that confront the past-life researcher.

Charles S—

This short life came up several times under hypnosis, and during the 1980s I tried to find out more about it. Initially, I think my concerns about following up a memory that was not remembered spontaneously may have hampered my investigation. Past-life memory recovered under hypnosis does not have the immediate reality of memories that arise naturally during childhood; as adults we are inclined to make subjective observations that alter our perception, so that any core of accurate detail become lost in a sea of additions. However, as the life had taken place relatively recently, between 1940 and 1945, it was reasonable to believe that it might be traceable.

Under hypnosis, I gave the name as Charles S—; I could not remember the full surname. Because I was looking at my surroundings from the point of view of a six-year-old child, it seemed at first that there was very little useful detail to go on. However, over time I began to realise that there were some strong key points, and a good chance of following these up. First, I had to sift through everything and whittle the clues down to the few that seemed clearest.

There was no father present, which would not be unusual in wartime; I had a strong feeling that he was not going to return, so I was probably looking for a child whose father had died in the war. When asked the father's name, I thought it might be Raymond. My memories were of a self-contained, rather lonely child who spent most of the time on his own, either in the area in front of the house or in the garden, which had at least one mature tree and offered a view of the house, possibly semidetached, and suggesting late-Victorian architecture.

Indoors, the family spent their time mainly in the kitchen at the back, of which I was able to give quite a detailed description. It had a side entrance to the left of the house, and on that side were some outbuildings – possibly a coal shed, and perhaps a separate outbuilding in the back garden. I thought there were two rooms at the front, the one more often used being on the left facing the house.

Almost opposite the house there was a side road going slightly uphill. The route Charles most frequently took, holding his mother's hand, was downhill to a crossroads where I could see a street sign. I described a school that was reached by going down the road, turning right and crossing over. Charles would play a game at the roadside, one foot on and one foot off the pavement, hopping up and down the kerb. The road was virtually empty of cars.

One of the things that threw me off course the first time I tried to follow up the case was that Jim, the hypnotist, asked me to look at the street sign, and I came up with two letters, NE. To me, as adult observer, this meant north London. As a result, I ended up on a wild-goose chase in Hendon. I also saw that the street name had a double-L in it. Here I made another mistake: by using logic rather than intuition, I decided this might be part of the word 'Hill'. Looking at a map of Hendon I found a Hill Crest, which led me even further astray. When I went there, it looked completely wrong. The problem was that I was seeing the words from the point of view of a small boy who was a virtual nonreader. Going back to basics, all I actually saw was the double-L.

Clearly, starting with the location was not going to produce results. I decided to try looking up deaths for the time period concerned, with a few years either side to be quite certain. I would look at all the children who had died at about the right age, certainly under nine, and list all those whose first name was Charles.

My mother helped with the search; she booked a day at the Record Office in Hertford and helped me search painstakingly through the microfiche records on a screen. Several trips and many hours took us up to the end of 1945 and revealed only one Charles S— who was alive at the right time and died aged six in 1945. I ordered a birth certificate for the child and discovered he was actually born in Gateshead. I checked the address against an old *A–Z* of Newcastle and Gateshead, but the road layout for the address given on the birth certificate was quite wrong, and I decided to abandon the search.

Several years later, however, it occurred to me that the family might have moved, and I could check this by ordering a death certificate. When it came, my hunch had been right. When I checked the new address on the old *A–Z*, the road layout looked familiar, and things began to slot into place.

The date of death was 19 October 1945 (coincidentally, Mary Sutton had also died in October). There was one surprise. Previously, I had thought that Charles had died of some kind of fever – I remembered, or thought I remembered, his illness. This is perhaps an instance of my producing an inaccurate answer under hypnosis in the desire to answer a specific question. Charles's death certificate told a different story: he had been run over by a lorry in the street outside his home. This explained a previously inexplicable memory: when I was five or six I used to have a repeated nightmare in which I was pursued by a vehicle and struck down in the street outside my house.

At the time, Charles was living in a less central part of Gateshead, in Elliot Road – hence the double L. The road layout was remarkably similar to my memory, including the position of the primary school, which was clearly marked. In the intervening years the father had died, presumably in the war. The area was close to the river valley, so any downward incline, however slight, would be in the direction of the river and the school.

Although all this seemed to match, I was still cautious,

CERTIFIED COPY of an
Pursuant to the Births and

ENTRY OF DEATH
Deaths Registration Act 1953

Registration District Gateshead

Death in the Sub-district of Gateshead Second in the County Borough of Gateshead

1945.								
Columns:-	1	2	3	4	5	6	7	8	9
No.	When and where died	Name and surname	Sex	Age	Occupation	Cause of death	Signature, description, and residence of informant	When registered	Signature of registrar
■	Nineteenth October 1945 Elliott Road Gateshead	Charles Hardwicke S■	Male	6 years	Son of Charles Edward S■ deceased a General labourer of Elliott Road.	Injuries accidentally sustained as a result of being run over by a motor lorry. No P.M.	Certificate received from William Carr Coroner for the West Chester Ward of Durham Inquest hold on the 22nd October 1945 and by adjournment on the 26th Nov 1945	Twenty Sixth November 1945	John Cowie
									Registrar.

Certified to be a true copy of an entry in a register in my custody.

_____ Superintendent Registrar

13 Aug 02 Date

Charles's death certificate

and it was some time before I picked up the research again. Eventually, however, early in 2005, I wrote to the current owner of the house asking about the family who had lived there in 1945, and also about the position of the house on the street.

I was lucky enough to receive a helpful reply straightaway. I was told that the house was on the correct side of the road, almost facing another road, just as I remembered. My perception of its age was probably right, because I was told that the area was being extensively developed and old houses had already been pulled down in the surrounding streets – it seemed I was lucky to find it still standing.

Brian Thomas, a local man who had read *Yesterday's Children*, kindly offered to look at the house while he was visiting Newcastle in August 2005. He found it pretty much as I had described: quite large, double-fronted, with a side entrance to the left and a front door in the middle. Although the road had a very slight incline, it was virtually flat. I had also written to the school marked in the old map, but had had no reply. Brian was able to tell me that there were now two fairly new schools, neither of them in the right location, whereas the old school had been.

It took time to realise it, but it did look as though I had found the right location for Charles S— in Gateshead. I wondered about trying to trace family members, but in this case I really did not have the heart. If Charles's mother was still living she would be in her late eighties. She had lost her husband in the war and her young son shortly afterwards; I did not think it would be right to tell her about my memories.

After about a year, I considered tracing her if I could; if she was no longer alive, I could release the surname. However, there was a problem: if she was living, I could not explain why I was trying to trace her. I wrote to several people with the right surname who were listed in the Gateshead telephone directory; I had some kind replies, but no news of the lady. I considered going back to the Hertford Record Office to check marriage and death records from 1945 to the present day, but the time involved would have been enormous. I had to accept that, although I had traced Charles's life, I would not be able to release his surname.

Jane Matthews

While I was in the final stages of researching the Japanese life, another memory suddenly became persistent. Over the August Bank Holiday weekend of 2006 I passed a fairground organ that was playing an old folk tune that I recognised as a marching song often used during the American Civil War. Although I had heard it before, this version included a distinctive, high-pitched piccolo strand, which struck me to the heart. Deeply affected, I had to walk away. Images arose of someone, a young man, leaving me to march off to war, and knowing that I would never see him again.

This was difficult. I had no desire to start the whole process of searching for a past life all over again, but at the same time I was well aware how much I felt driven to do so. Thinking about it, I immediately discounted any American Civil War connection and started looking for another association. My closest friend had had many years' involvement with English Civil War re-enactment and had a better grasp of history than I; she was also a keen equestrian. When I asked if she knew anything about the music she pinpointed it as a cavalry piece probably used from about 1800. This gave me a time-frame to work with.

Under hypnosis I had recalled a life as a girl in Southampton, roughly between the 1830s and 1850s (I describe it in Chapter 4). Among the fragmented images, I could never see myself as older than a teenager; I remembered leaving home, very upset, and dying while sheltering in a barn.

I remembered sailing ships with tall masts, and had quite a strong image of small, squalid backstreets with cramped terrace houses. In our home in one of these narrow streets, the whole family seemed to spend the day crammed into one room, so the house may have been very small. I could see my mother with a basket of laundry, which she may have taken in to earn money, and I had sisters. I felt that I was the oldest girl in a reasonably large family.

From our home, I remembered walking down a long road to the quayside area where ships were unloaded and spending time with a young man friend gleaning spilled cargo. A few years ago I had heard that the people living in dockside areas in those days would often pick up stray oddments of spilled cargo; it was not considered theft, as damaged cargo would otherwise be spoiled or claimed by the tide. This information helped to strengthen my confidence in the memory.

So now I was looking for a war that could have recruited my young man friend close to the end of Jane's lifetime in the early 1850s. The Crimean War, starting in 1854, fitted perfectly. One of the memories triggered by the marching tune was of standing on a crowded pavement watching men marching through the town, lots of men, while the tune was played on a piccolo and drums. I seemed to be very thin and poorly dressed; I stood at the back of the crowd, not daring to push to the front to get a better view. The marching conscripts looked equally scruffy, although many of them wore uniform jackets.

To reach the Crimean Peninsula, which juts out into the Black Sea, British ships would have had to travel south through the Mediterranean, then through the Aegean, round Turkey to squeeze through the Sea of Marmara and the Bosporus Strait to reach the Black Sea. It is very likely that most of the British ships were dispatched from the large, southern port of Southampton.

Unlike with some of my other memories, I had no clear sense of location. My recall of the local streets was sketchy at best: all I could remember were the few streets around my home and walking to the quayside. A modern map of Southampton showed no road layout that I could recognise, so I wrote to a museum in Southampton in the hope that they might know of an old map or history book I could acquire.

Then, quite by chance, I found a book of maps of British towns between 1800 and 1855, exactly the right time slot. Among the fifty-six towns included there was an old map of Southampton. This was wonderful! I was looking at a map showing how the tiny, densely built-up streets clustered around the dock and quay areas. The town used to finish at Western Shore Road (now Western Esplanade), Canute Road and the docks, and on the east side at Albert Marine Parade by the wharfs. It was now clear why modern maps had made no sense to me: there had been considerable expansion of the dock area and land reclamation around the town's coast. Many of the small roads had been replaced with shopping

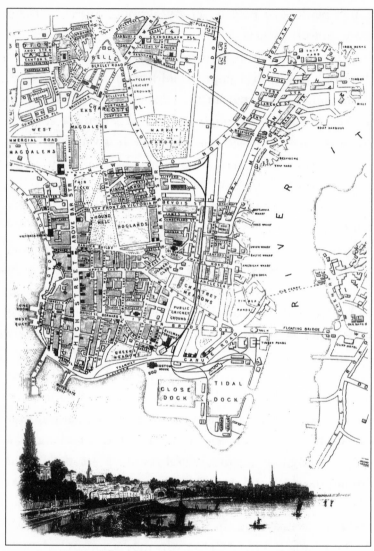

Map of Southampton, c.1800–55

centres, car parks and industrial areas; others had been radically changed or had disappeared.

In my memory I was certain that I could walk to the end of a long road to the docks close by; I could see the tall ships and the wide area where the cargo was unloaded. I remembered seeing bales of cotton stacked on the quayside. Walking down the road towards the sea, I sensed that most of the town and dock area was to my left, so I should be searching in the western part of the town.

Then I received a response to my letter to the museum, which had been passed to the Southampton Reference Library: a copy of an 1842 map. This was rather more detailed, even if somewhat less clear.

Under hypnosis I had given the name for this lifetime as Jane, possibly Jane Matthews. I am only too aware that surnames are the weakest spot in my otherwise rather effective memory, and this weakness is liable to be more apparent when I am using hypnosis. However, with Charles I had at least remembered the first letter of his surname, so it was worth starting my research with the name Matthews.

My next step was to telephone the reference library, asking to see the Southampton census records for 1851 and 1861; if Jane appeared on the first and not the second, this could indicate her death during the intervening years – although it could also mean that she had moved away or married. I had to leave my details with the reference library office, as the records were not open for public research.

Further reading showed that the population of Southampton increased sixfold between 1801 and 1861, which could explain the sense of being overcrowded. The city saw enormous expansion during this period, in all kinds of manufacturing industry as well as shipping.

After a few days a lady rang back from Southampton Reference Library having found census records for a Jane Matthews living in the tiny streets to the west of the town in 1851. In fact there were two Jane Matthewses listed, but one could be discounted. She was too old – eighteen in 1851 – and not born in Southampton, which seemed wrong. She was also the only one to appear in the 1861 census, as a twenty-eight-year-old housemaid living with her mother.

The other Jane Matthews was thirteen in 1851, just the right age, and did not appear in the 1861 census, which was encouraging. She was also the oldest daughter, but had only two sisters, which would make the family smaller than I remembered. Also, she lived rather further from the docks, and not quite as far west as I recalled – in Craven Street near West Front, where there were a number of narrow backstreets. There was no father listed, but the mother was recorded as married, wife to the head of the household. In Jane's life I had memories of paternal violence occurring intermittently, which would fit with a father who worked away for some of the time. The mother was a stay maker by occupation, which could explain my memory of a laundry or clothes basket.

Quite a lot fitted, and it seemed worth checking a bit further. My next task was to try to find records and deaths and marriages for the period – if Jane had married, she could not be the Jane of my memory. But if there was a record of death between 1851 and 1861, she could be the right girl.

Once again my mother and I visited the Hertford Record Office, but could find no record of death for Jane Matthews during the relevant period. Nor could we find any marriage details for those years. Records from that period are very difficult to read, especially on microfiche, but we were quite certain that we had found nothing. There was more research to be done.

It was possible that the family had moved away before the 1861 census. The librarian at the Southampton Library kindly tracked down the movements of the family. Alas, we were on the wrong trail. From the records, it was clear that the family had moved to Kensington.

This was not the end. I considered other ways of continuing the search. In every other case I had tried to research I had failed to supply a full or correct surname, but had been accurate about the first name, location, facets of historical data and, particularly, many small details relating to the home. Now I would have to go back to basics; assuming that I could not rely on the surname I would have to approach the problem from a new direction.

It was a matter of statistics. Even without a surname, if there were enough correct details, the truth of the case became more likely. With Mary Sutton I had compiled nine pages of correct information, far too much for coincidence, and each time I saw Sonny more facts were confirmed. With Charles the facts were few, but the memory was still accurate as far as it went. As for the Japanese memory, there were so many specific details about the location that my description would not have matched any other site in Japan, while the social information fixed it in time, even without confirmatory records.

In Jane's case I had only a few details to check. First, the location: partway down the east side of a street in west

Southampton that ran directly to the shore. It looked from the old map to be probably French Street or Bugle Street, or possibly West Place. There were some historical details to match the time in history. The first name was probably reliable, and could be used in the search. The size of the family was usual for the times, but Jane's being the oldest girl might be helpful.

I was beginning to realise that, even if I found a match, there were far too few details to make a convincing case. However, I still needed to settle my sense of unrest and decided to spend a little more time on it. Logic suggested that the best course would be to find census records for the specific streets and look for a Jane of the right age who was present in the 1851 census but not in 1861. If I could find a name I could then search for a death certificate.

However, this would involve looking through the whole census for Southampton to find the right streets. I tried to do this by accessing Internet sites, but this was time-consuming and unsatisfactory. Most sites are set up for family research and assume that the surname is known. I could not find one that would allow me to view street by street. In addition, many of the sites ask for payment for a service that does not guarantee results. After spending hours at my computer getting nowhere, I abandoned the Internet.

So, to other ideas. If I could organise a free day for a trip to London, I could go to the Family Records Centre in Myddleton Street, which had taken over from the old Somerset House venue. But first I could enlist help from the local library to see if their service was offered somewhere closer. After all my trips to Hertford in the past, I felt slightly foolish when I discovered that microfiche records were offered by the main library in Northampton, barely ten miles away. Once I had found a name or names, I could book time there to look up dates of death. However, they held only local census details, so I would have to look further afield for national figures.

The Northampton council office that had directed me to the library also gave me the address of the Family Research Centre at a fairly local Mormon church, which turned out to hold copies of all the censuses. There, in March 2007, I managed to check through the entire 1851 census for South-ampton to locate a girl in the right area, of the right age and the right first name. It was a mammoth task. There were about sixty Janes in the right age group in Southampton at the time, about a third of them in the right part of the city.

I started to cross-check some of the addresses against the 1861 census, but many of the families had moved. Using this method was not going to work. To make matters worse, several of the surnames were indecipherable owing to poor handwriting and degradation of the records. In all the other memories I had researched I had had a very specific location for the home, which at least had given me an immutable constant to work around. I now realised that without it the task was nearly impossible.

Past-life memories are very personal and affect the way we feel, our responses and reactions to various stimuli. But, without a statistically valid quantity of confirmable details, the memory alone cannot provide the evidence needed. I had to recognise that I was spending too much time and effort hunting down a memory that was too light on detail.

As one final effort, I booked a microfiche session at the public library and spent some time looking through death records just in case I got lucky. It turned out to be a thankless task. The records for those years were handwritten and gave no age at death. I had to concede that, even if I were to spend several weeks full time on the search, I simply did not have enough information to complete it. Even if I found a match, it would not be statistically valid, nor would it be precise enough to satisfy my desire for completion.

Finally, the death may not have occurred in Southampton, and the name may never have been recorded. A young runaway girl, dying alone in a barn, may have been impossible to identify. There was the possibility of searching through old newspaper archives for a report of her death – but this, too, could be time-consuming and less than useful. This time my obsessive persistence would not be enough: I would have to let Jane go, drifting into her lonely, unrecorded death among the straw and the horses.

INDEX

Note: page numbers in **bold** refer to maps/figures.